The Essence of Education

Robert Astwood

Copyright © 2021 by Robert Astwood

All rights reserved. No part of this book may be reproduced or used in any manner without written permission of the copyright owner except for the use of quotations in a book review.

For more information, email: astwood@astereducation.net
Instagram: @aster_education

First paperback edition November 2021
Printed in the United States of America

ISBN 978-0-578-99653-0 (paperback)

www.astwood@astereducation.net

About the Author

Hailing from the Bronx, NY, Robert Astwood is a staunch advocate for systemic school change and education reform. On a mission to positively impact the lives of 400 million people, his personal calling is to uproot the neoliberal school system and rebuild it on altruism, interdependence, and the whole person-approach. At the time of publication, Robert educates the youth as a life enrichment coach where he mentors children aged 10-18 at Elevate Education and The Wise Institute. When he is not engaging the student community, he spends his spare time hosting a podcast on school change and he also creates life education content on social media. Robert's big-think vision is to open 10 schools in all 50 states of the U.S. with the intention of shifting national focus away from production and division in schools to an environment that actively promotes the authentic development of the full human person

Acknowledgments

Before we get started, I just wanted to thank my family for providing me with the physical, mental, and spiritual resources that shaped me into the person I am today. More specifically, I thank my mother, grandmother, my aunt, my brother, and my niece. I always say that I am an eclectic combination of all of them. They each add nuances to my personality and I am so grateful to have been supported by them. Because of their love, mentorship, and support, I am able to share this book with you. So thank you for all you have done and all you will do, it is greatly appreciated. And now, let's get to our feature presentation! Enjoy!

Table of Contents

Chapter 1 – Introduction to Education   1

Chapter 2 – Un-education of the Youth   4

Chapter 3 – Education as Improvement   8

Chapter 4 – Activity? Or Mindset?   13

Chapter 5 – Aspects of Education   20

- Education as Knowledge?
- Defense from Deceit
- Education as Customization

Chapter 6 – Essentials of Education   29

- Insight Exposure
- Real-World Experience
- Official Schooling
- Self-Teaching
- Acquisition of Values

Chapter 7 – Learning   41

- Memory
- Focus and Desire

- Sense Learning
- Drawing Connections
- Vicarious Learning
- Trial, Error, Praxis
- Difference Between Teaching and Learning

Chapter 8 – Active Involvement, Hunting Will, Focus   66

Chapter 9 – Education as Practical Comprehension   70

Chapter 10 – Progress   75

Chapter 11 – Failure   84

- Failure as Instruction
- Failure as Recollection
- Fear of Failure
- Failure as Fuel

Chapter 12 – Humanization and Organic Intelligence   95

- Life Enrichment
- Place-Based Learning
- Altruism
- Whole-Person Approach
- Application of Ability

Closing Thoughts   107

Preface

Greetings cultivators of the future and welcome to the Essence of Education! First, I want to thank you for your purchase, you are indubitably in for a wild ride!

To be clear, I created this book with three main intentions:

1. To show why and how schools should and **must** change for the benefit of **all** stakeholders.

2. To shift the way we conceive education, teaching, and learning while adding on to what is considered worth including in our curriculum.

3. To disrupt the current norms of education while suggesting our solution lies in founding schools on altruism, interdependence, and the whole-person approach.

This book is intended to help you as teachers, school leaders, and parents to reflect on your current approach to education with the intention of improving your understanding of your learners as well as your ability to cultivate their full humanity. In addition to discussing the essence of education, you will be asked to actively participate with this book. For this to provide the most benefit, I have included short activities at the end of each chapter with some space to be filled out by you. In addition, I encourage you to have a small notebook or legal pad to accompany you while you read this book as you may find that you wish to keep track of your answers. Using it in this journal format will help you reflect on your own current practices and determine how to enhance your approach to better suit the needs of your learners. Warning: This interactive book will only net you positive results if and ONLY if you actively engage with the text and diligently complete each activity to the best of your ability. This is a space of acceptance, creativity, and brainstorming. My main reason for these activities is to get you to relate the insights presented in the text to your own life experience with the goal of implementing new understandings right away. In addition, it is my intent to guide you toward actively applying insights from our discussion to find fresh solutions to our contemporary problems.

Final note on the activities, each of these has specific functions and some are designed strictly for educators while some encompass both teachers and students. Some of these challenges, such as Fight the Fear in chapter 11, may require the educator to first master the activity themself before introducing it to their learners.

Since I understand and value your time as teachers, educators, and school leaders, this text is designed to engage you efficiently and effectively. As an added bonus, I even made this a short read! Just over 100 pages, this is jam-packed with thoughts and perspectives amalgamated from thinkers like John Dewey, Jean Jacques Rousseau, Gert Biesta, and Carol Dweck. Given my studies in Teachers College, Columbia University and my own personal experience, I have come to my own eclectic approach to education which I term Humanization and Organic Intelligence (HOI) which I introduce later in this work. Ultimately, the purpose of this book is to question the commonly accepted notions of what is considered education and strive to add more scope, depth, and versatility to the notions of education, teaching, and learning. In addition, it is my authentic promise to you to add value to your lives and provide you with increased ability to cultivate yourselves and your learners.

So let's get started! ShowTime!

Chapter 1

Introduction to Education: What is it?

America is failing our youth. With the heavy focus on ranking, tracking, irrelevant class content, teach-to-test, and banking style education, students are divested of the opportunity to develop their full human capacities. For too long, our nation has overlooked the essential qualities of education resulting in the widespread creation of factory workers and egocentric individuals. If this climate of neoliberal schooling continues, it can spell trouble for the future of our nation. It doesn't take much to see this trouble in action. In our recent generation of college graduates ranging from 2015-2021, many young adults find themselves returning home with parents after graduating. Another number of students are stuck at dead-end jobs after receiving their diploma in an unrelated field of study. Yet another percentage of students are drifting along with no real purpose, simply achieving the goals of others. In addition, with the focus on ranking and competition, upon leaving school students are programmed to see their peers as opponents rather than team players, only serving to further divide us as humans. This holds true for the workplace, friend groups, and the like. This is certainly a far cry from what we are truly capable of as human beings. In our increasingly changing environment, our 21st-century world needs thought leaders, change agents, inventors, and innovators. Yet, our current school system only grooms learners for production, consumption, and regulations. Anyone who wishes a wider path needs to work for it on their own. This fact is simply an injustice on the part of schools and can stand no longer. For students to invest so much time into school to gain only limited human development is larceny and must be ceased immediately.

Consequently, I have crafted this book to shift our national awareness away from production and competition. It is my fervent belief that we as a nation must instead focus on cultivating the full humanity of each and every stakeholder in education. To achieve this will require us to place altruism, interdependence, and the whole-person approach as the foundation of education. This will be actualized using principles known as Humanization and Organic Intelligence (HOI), a concept that will be introduced in the final chapter of this book. To begin this journey, let's explore the notion of education and expand its reach.

What do you think of when you hear the word 'education'? What concepts, images, or experiences are conjured in your mind? One immediate reaction to this question may yield a response such as "Education is going to school, reading books, and attaining knowledge" or "education is learning." While these answers aren't wrong, education and what it involves can be further described. Aside from attending classes, studying for exams, and taking standardized tests, education expands outside the realm of the classroom. Education extends into your daily experience and – provided it is utilized - it affects how well you perform in life and society. To clarify, when I say 'education' I am not referring only to official schooling for there are profuse examples of individuals that have achieved high levels of education in their life without attending university classes. When I say education, I am describing the process you undergo in order to improve yourself while discovering your humanity and relation to yourself, the world, and others. Schooling is merely one of the ways to gain this improvement. So to get started, the following activity will ask that you include your view on education in the space provided.

See you there!

Hey! Glad you could make it!

Activity: Declaration of Education

At this point, what does education mean to you? How has education been portrayed in your life? At this moment, what is the purpose of education in your eyes? Write your responses down in the space below. Keep it close to you as it will be helpful for you to have these notions in mind as we move along in this book.

_____

_____

_____

_____

_____

_____

_____

_____

_____

_____

Chapter 2

Education vs. Official Schooling: The Un-Education of the Youth

Before moving any further, I do want to iterate this drastic difference between education and schooling. Often, we tend to hear these terms used interchangeably, however this is a dangerous practice to engage in. The etymological root of the word educate derives from the Latin 'educatus' which means to bring up, to draw out, or bring forth. In our contemporary dictionaries, educate refers to the development of the faculties or powers of a person. From these descriptions, it appears that the word educate implies to progress or get better in some form or fashion. This is the crux of education, improvement and forward movement. Hence, this *should* be the goals of our schools, however current practices suggest otherwise. Given that schools prioritize other items before the improvement factor, they stand as locations of severe un-education. The manner in which schools are executed now mainly serve to un-educate learners, as well as other education stakeholders i.e., teachers, parents, and school leaders. So what do I mean by the term un-educate? Very simply, this refers to limiting and preventing one's ability or desire to improve. Schools strip kids of these desires in a myriad of ways but here are a few examples: standardized testing, irrelevant classroom content, lack of inclusion, promotion of limiting beliefs, and so much more. Respectively, the aforementioned items un-educate kids through: discouragement, lack of intellectual engagement, segregation, and fixed mindset. For example, just consider a child in a classroom learning about historical facts from the 16th century. Not only is the information boring and unapplicable to the student's life, often the information is delivered in a rote and dry manner, using the lecture style pedagogy. In short, contemporary schooling is less a place of education and more a place of limited indoctrination. Sounds strange? Think of it this way, if education is improvement and progression, schools are a place of social programming and training. It teaches you a truncated view of the world and only gives you two ways to exist in that world, as a worker and a follower. However, schools are not programming our students for altruism, interdependence, or personal greatness. Unfortunately, schools are preparing our youth to be banal, dependent, divisive, and focused on consumption. Hence, this is the un-education to which I refer. In terse terms, un-education refers to limited beliefs, disarray, and lack of progression.

Whew that was heavy! How about we loosen up with an exercise?

Let's do this!

Activity: Un-Education in Action

In your experience in education, name three times that you have seen this un-education in action. Be specific!

    1.

    2.

    3.

Now, considering your previously written purpose of education, what are three ways that you would work to change this in your school or education experience? Would you start at the curriculum? School policies? Community initiatives? How would you actively strive to ensure the interdependence, altruism, and full humanity of your students is consistently cultivated? I encourage you to share your brainstorms with your fellow educators, friends, or colleagues as you may find that together you will discover even more creative solutions to this issue.

1.

2.

3.

Chapter 3

Education as Improvement: Micro and Macro

Think of the various people that have achieved high levels of success with limited or zero higher education experience. On this list would be people like Bill Gates, Steve Jobs, Mark Zuckerberg, and Rachel Ray. And this list could go on and on. However, despite not possessing a formal education, these people are not devoid of education altogether. They simply focused on a particular field and gained improvements in their own way. In fact, these individuals have some of the richest education in their respective field. Steve Jobs had massive education in the area of technology, which is why he was able to innovate in the way he did. If he didn't know how to create various computer programs, it is unlikely he would have the ability to create an item like the iPhone. Take a superstar athlete; say it's Lebron. He is profusely educated in the field of basketball, so much so that he dominates his sector with his deep knowledge of the inner workings of the game. And how is this knowledge achieved? If you were to ask Lebron, he may reply with something like "lots of hard work and practice" or maybe something like "a hell of a lot of trial and error." And these responses would certainly be items involved in the education process. It's a simple notion, education involves hard work, practice, and learning from your mistakes in order to become better in the given field. In addition, it relies heavily on firsthand experience. In order to gain a true frame of reference, we must create personal experiences to draw from. This is a huge area that our contemporary schools overlook with current teach-to-test models that fetter us to impractical material. Overall, to achieve expertise in any given area one must become deeply educated in that field of inquiry. This study and development of one discipline is the first mode of education that I refer to as Micro Education. Micro Education denotes one's specialized craft. For example, as a person who draws blood, my micro education would be phlebotomy. Or if I am one that instructs students, my micro education would be that of a teacher. Say I am in the business of taking photos for a newspaper; my micro education would be news photographer.

Analogous to education in specific fields, this concept of education is present in one's comportment and overall mental disposition during everyday life. Practicing to be a more successful human being is tantamount to achieving success in a specialized field. This type of education refers to one's general knowledge, ability, and ways of engaging in the world. This version of education would involve new ways of conveying and understanding information, creating and evolving one's perception of the world, and improving the way one communicates with others. In addition, it entails how to effectively react when given certain variables, seeing problems as opportunities for growth, and maximizing one's resources for success. These are all areas of education that are often overlooked because of the focus on official schooling. The ideas that I am attempting to capture here are all part of what I term Macro Education. This type of education usually **cannot be taught directly via methods of instruction**, rather they must be inspired and encouraged within a learner - by an exposer of knowledge - on their own terms and for their own reasons. Macro Education encompasses broader, more abstract abilities. Think of the person that is good at reading body language, or that fellow that can seamlessly interact with a variety of people of conflicting backgrounds. Or maybe it's the person that is constantly looking for life lessons in situations while maintaining a positive outlook. Most importantly, it is how well the person can synergize their accumulated knowledge and understanding of the world and how to use it effectively and appropriately according to the given context. This is similar to the concept mentioned by educational psychologist Raymond Cattell, "Fluid general ability…shows more in tests requiring adaptation to new situations…the form of fluid ability…is due to an influence present and operative at the time of the experiment" (Cattell, 1963). Macro education can be thought of as the use of one's general abilities based off a certain context or situation, similar to Cattell's notion of fluid intelligence. However, unlike Cattell implies in his work, macro education is not biologically determined. Rather, like a skill, it is something that can be practiced and further developed. The main takeaway here would be the ability to adjust and interact with one's environment while actively seeking to improve this method of interaction. An individual with high macro education tends to exhibit qualities of creativity, growth mindset, and ingenuity. Each of these attributes that I am describing are various things not taught in official schooling but are skills that are crucial to being a human in today's society. These two types of education can be thought in terms of a resume with hard skills and soft skills: micro education represents an individual's hard skills and macro education signifies one's soft skills. Finally, it is important to note that we should refrain from limiting ourselves to only one of these camps. In order to become fully human, it is necessary to scale both of these capacities to our greatest ability while using both to feed one another harmoniously.

Activity: As you were reading, you may have already been thinking of some of your own micro and macro abilities. So this exercise will be 2-fold. First, I want you to reflect on your own abilities and write down 2 for each.

Micro	Macro

Then, I want you to consider your students. What are things they are good at? What unique skills do they possess? What are some fluid intelligence capacities they exhibit that perhaps you overlooked? This exercise is designed to get you thinking of your students in terms of what they CAN do, refraining from labeling them by what they cannot.

Your Student's Skills

Micro	Macro

Chapter 4

Education: An Activity? A Mindset? Or Both?

Education can be treated in two ways. It can be viewed as an activity, something that is conducted for an allotted period of time, or as a mindset, something that is constantly occurring. The way in which it is perceived depends on the person's outlook of education.

Education as an activity is when someone engages in education as a transient occurrence. Envision yourself attending the latest release of a popular movie franchise. You go there with your friend, you order the popcorn, and make your way to the theater. You sit down, recline, and wait for the movie to begin. For the next two hours you are experiencing an alternate reality; you are fully engaged in a focused activity. Once the movie is complete, you exit the theater and return to your routine life. Just like how we briefly experience the activity of watching that film, we also can briefly engage in an activity of education. We can show up to the 'theater of education' and passively or actively learn new concepts.[1] This process could last just 5-10 minutes, or 2-3 hours depending on how much time one chooses to dedicate to that activity. Once the session is complete, we leave the theater of education. We shut off the portion of our mind that is linked to that particular area of study until it is time to learn more on the subject at a later session. Conducting one's education in this manner is beneficial in that it yields results. When studying a given topic in allotted periods of time, one is able to acquire knowledge on facts of the subject. In effect, education as an activity does enable us to learn. Through this method, we are

---

[1] The theater of education refers to the physical location in which learning takes place. These areas vary and are not limited to any one specific area. eg. Library, home, school, mall, etc.

able to gain knowledge of concepts to a certain extent. However, using this view of education can hinder how well one can truly know about that topic. To augment one's knowledge further, there is another attitude that one can adopt which I will refer to as education as a mindset or 'engage education'. In looking at education as something that you live by on a daily and spontaneous basis, it can provide a richer experience for the learner. Education as a mindset implies one is in a constant state of learning or one is consistently ready to improve at any moment. Their mind is not shut off from the idea of education and they are constantly poised to gain new information of any given phenomenon in their experience. It is because of this ongoing desire for improvement that I call this way of looking at education 'engage education' because this person is usually ready to interact with new information and is constantly tuned in to learn new lessons. When viewed as an activity, I term this allotted education. I describe it in this manner because this type of person sets aside times to improve themselves on a particular routine or schedule. Most importantly, I look at these approaches as mental outlooks that determine a person's thoughts and actions. To further describe the two outlooks, here are some examples of phrases that you will hear from each mindset camp respectively.

Allotted: "That's just how things are" "Why would I want to do that now? This isn't school!" "There's a time and place for education". The main point here is that a person with this worldview limits how much they can truly learn in natural moments because they feel their education is reserved for the schoolhouse or some other designated area.

Engage: "Where is the lesson here?" "How can I use this situation to gain new insight?" "How can I apply what I have been learning to this current situation?" The main point here is that this individual focuses on creating life lessons from thin air using the given situation as a catalyst.

Although these methods are both advantageous in improving one as a person, I prefer to advocate for engage education because this way of perceiving education can yield stronger results when it comes to knowledge acquisition and improvement. Furthermore, viewing the need to self-improve as non-negotiable makes one more inclined to become better.

The two types of education - micro and macro - and the two outlooks on education -engage and allotted - are useful components in gaining a comprehensive view of what education entails. However, they are auxiliary factors in regard to education. In the next sections, the necessary and sufficient conditions of education will be explored. The necessary condition refers to a quality that a given noun needs in order to be considered that given thing. In other words, if fire did not produce light or heat it would not be considered fire for it does not meet the necessary conditions. Likewise, if water was dry, it would not be water. Therefore, the necessary condition is an essential quality that a given noun needs in order to be considered that given noun. Lateral to this is the sufficient conditions of something. This involves the coincidental truths about that thing such as its height, weight, length, shape, etc. For instance, a pencil can be any color, width, height, or length. It can write darker and lighter lines. It can be a mechanical pencil or standard. These facts are all sufficient qualities of the pencil. They have small effect on the necessary function of the pencil which is to write lines on paper. The necessary condition of the pencil is simply to write and erase when needed, nothing more. While the color and size of the pencil may vary depending on the desired task, these sufficient qualities do not prevent the pencil from achieving its necessary condition of writing. Analogous to the concept of necessary and sufficient conditions of the pencil, these same conditions apply to education as well. The sufficient condition of education will be referred to as the aspects of education while the necessary conditions will be regarded as the essentials of education.

On the following page you will find a quick quiz to further your understanding of micro and macro education.

Welcome to the Engage Station! Get ready!

Activity: Allotted Education vs. Engage Education

Quiz time! Below you will find various scenarios. Your job is super simple, all you need to do is choose which outlook best fits the situation. Choose whether or not you think each scenario is an allotted or engage approach. This is to add more depth to your understanding of the two and the qualifiers of each.

1. Laura is currently taking Spanish 101. This is the first time that she has ever taken a foreign language class and she is feeling a bit shy, but confident she can learn the new skill. After taking classes for a few days, she begins to practice a few vocabulary drills outside of class time. Along with this, she has also purchased additional vocabulary books and practice drills, unprompted by the teacher. Laura also strives to actively use the new language with her bilingual friends, and any Spanish-speaking servers she encounters at restaurants.

    Which approach is Laura operating with?

    A: Allotted Education   B: Engage Education

2. Vanessa just recently purchased a new online training course on digital marketing that claimed to teach on how to monetize social media. After exploring the course for a few hours, she realizes that the bulk of the information is really just packed with a bunch of testimonials without any specific advice on how to achieve her desired goal. Though disappointed, she notices something about the testimonials that, in her mind, hindered their overall credibility. Since she one day hopes to own her own business with a plethora of clients, she begins to look at this situation as an opportunity to inform her personal

goal. She uses this instance as a chance to learn about what she will do when she starts filming testimonials of her own.

Which approach is Vanessa using?

A: Allotted Education   B: Engage Education

3. David just recently started a new position at a direct marketing company. The job is focused on learning how to build and operate a business while conducting door-to-door sales for Verizon Fios. In order to move up in the job, it is necessary for David to master sales and then develop/manage a small team of people. As per his job description, David carries out the required tasks such as calling on clients, attending meetings, and closing deals with prospects. When it is time to clock out, he goes home to unwind, putting work on the back-burner of his mind.

Which approach is David operating on?

A: Allotted Education   B. Engage Education

4. It's three months into the school year, and Ms. Cruz has been experiencing many hardships in her first year of teaching 6th grade. Despite these obstacles, she is constantly using her time outside of the classroom to improve on her weaknesses while increasing her strengths. She does this by watching videos on classroom management, reading books on developing authentic learning activities, and networking with veteran teachers. She makes it her mission to learn as much as she can so that she can constantly show up brighter, faster, and more effectively for her students. Her efforts far exceed those of the prescribed

professional development protocols provided by the school.

Which approach is Ms. Cruz using?

A: Allotted Education   B. Engage Education

5. Terry is a 9th grader reading a book on economics and she comes across a word that she is unfamiliar with. Since she will not be tested on this word and she won't need it for any particular classroom assignment, she continues on without conducting further inquiry on the word's meaning.

Which approach is she operating under?

A: Allotted Education   B: Engage Education

6. Jaylin has been together with his girlfriend for several months now. Things have been going well for the most part but every now and then the two experience arguments or disagreements. Often when this occurs, Jaylin finds that he is unsure of what to say, how to respond, or how to diffuse the situation. Finding this lack of knowledge disconcerting, he then makes it his duty to learn all he can about conflict management and understanding his romantic partner so that he is better equipped to handle future situations. The next time a crisis arises, he actively participates in utilizing the insight that he garnered during his personal research.

Which approach is Jaylin using?

A. Allotted Education   B: Engage Education

Chapter 5

Aspects of Education

Education as Knowledge?

In today's society, many people would agree with the old adage, knowledge is power. For years I blindly repeated this phrase and as I went through life's experiences, I kept striving to increase my knowledge. Only until recently did I begin to question the validity of this classic saying. I realized, just because you intellectually *know* a great deal of information doesn't mean that you can apply it effectively and accurately. I intellectually *know* that in order to be a more understanding person, I have to listen to others and make them feel heard before explaining my own viewpoint. However, this is extremely hard to implement in practice, especially in the heat of the moment. At times I still find myself interjecting before letting them finish or thinking about my own thoughts instead of theirs. Although I knew better, I still wasn't *doing* better. Today, I focus more on doing and less on knowing. Our contemporary school system holds a similar misguided belief in the conventional wisdom that knowledge is power. Today the words education, school, and knowledge are used almost synonymously. However, they are each nuanced items. As stated previously, the etymological root of education derives from the Latin 'educatus' which means to emerge from within or draw out. In my view, education means to bring out the improvement in another person. Schooling on the other hand, refers to the location designated for education to occur. This does not automatically mean that education occurs there, it is simply the designed space for that activity. Today, schools have been relegated to child factories where we are creating banal drones devoid of creativity, ambition, or interdependent motives. Knowledge refers to information known by an individual. The knowledge itself is not the power, rather it is the unique way in which the person uses the knowledge to benefit themselves, others, and the environment that holds true weight. Hence, knowledge is an aspect of education due to its role in informing a person or group. However the real essential quality, which will be explored later in greater detail, is one's practical comprehension or their ability to apply what they know.

Education as a Defense from Deceit

Let's face it. We or someone we know has been in a situation at some point where we were duped by someone simply because we were naïve and ignorant to a better course of action. Often, those who don't know better tend to fall victim to con-artists. They are taken advantage of by those more knowledgeable, resourceful, or influential. An instance of this is the history of the Catholic Church. During earlier time periods, many people were unable to read and write. Catholicism was a normative religion at the time and people wanted to ensure they would be granted good fortune and gain admission to heaven. People attended church and paid for absolution. In short, religion had an influence on the actions and beliefs of citizens. Since church figures are validated as messengers of God, this granted them an influence over others as well. With this religious credibility, priests were able to take advantage of the fickle populous and began to use religion to serve their own selfish ends. Since priests were cognizant of the desire of salvation and devotion to religion, they intentionally misinterpreted the bible. At the time, the bible was written in only Latin and being that the majority of people did not speak this language they were unable to refute the priest for heresy. As a result of this, they were exploited and the priests profited. This is a prime example of how the lack of education in a given field, in this case Latin, leaves one vulnerable to deceit.

Another example to illustrate this point will be shown in the interaction with a car mechanic. Think back to when you got your first car. It's an old 1999 Nissan Maxima that has 500,000+ miles. You're brand new to the road, and you still can't tell brake fluid from power-steering. You have zero knowledge of the inner workings of cars and after a few weeks of driving, you run into your first problem: your headlights stop working. Now for those of you that drive, you know that this is usually an easy fix - just go to an AutoZone and buy a head lamp - but being that this driver is brand new, they are unsure of what to do. For those who use the internet, they would probably just google their issue. However, let's consider that this person is one that does not "trust" or approve of the internet. Instead, they go over to the mechanic to solve their headlight problem. The mechanic, realizing that this person is brand new to the car scene, decides to take advantage of this new driver. What would normally cost $10-$15 ends up costing $50 because the new driver was uneducated in the realm of cars. And being that the novice doesn't know any better, he goes on thinking that head lamps for his car are $50 when they are in fact much cheaper. If he had education and experience in the field of mechanics, he would have been able to call the mechanic out for hiking the price. Hence, it stands to reason that education is a defense from deceit because it enables one to see through the haze that others purport as Truth.

So far, these have been examples of how the lack of education in a micro sense can lead to deceit. But how does this deception appear in a macro sense? To clarify, macro education refers to one's general knowledge, ability, and unique way of synergizing their current understanding of the world in a meaningful or beneficial way to themselves or others, while micro education refers to one's specialized craft. One's macro education can be described as the way one comports oneself based off the information believed to be intellectually and emotionally true. What this individual believes to be true is due largely in part to: the facticity they are born into and how well they apply themselves to learning new information. Not only is the former item more effectual in influencing a person's worldview, it sometimes affects how well that person chooses to apply themselves. Take the example of slavery, in any time period. Many slaves that were born into captivity never knew life outside of the grip of a master. As a slave, you are barred from all education; you are told that your sole existence is to serve others. Hearing this as a child and seeing each of your fellow slave members conform to this notion, you don't know any better. You are not educated to think otherwise, nor do you have the thought process to consider the possibility of something else. As a result, you grow up thinking that this is your existence. To you, you are just doing what you need to survive. Due to the lack of education, slaves unwittingly perpetuated this cycle. One key thing to note here is that while your environment can have a significant influence on you, it is not the ultimate determining factor of your success. This truth is seen in the gradual abolishment of slavery in the U.S. when the enslaved began to rise up and risk their lives for their freedom. This example of deceit due to lack of education can also be seen in the history of women in society. Throughout history, women have been objectified and relegated to nothing more than objects. Analogous to slaves, they too have been told a specific story since birth. Often society would inculcate into the minds of young girls that they are to remain quiet, look pretty, and serve the needs of men. In addition, they were also blocked from receiving education. With ideas like this instilled into them from birth, girls grew up into women that were constantly trying to please their husbands and provide for others. And without any education, they were made to remain in positions of submission. Hence, this stands as another way in which the lack of educational development can lead to the deceit and exploitation of others. Like with slavery in America, women in the U.S. have taken control of their subjectivity through action, education, and civil protest.

Education as Customization

This involves the ability to choose between various options. But if one is not privy to the options available then that individual is fettered to limited courses of action. Thus, this aspect of education involves being able to display versatility with a variety of situations they experience in life. Take for example, you have a chance of being promoted and your boss has invited you to golf. You are excited at the opportunity but there is just one small issue, you have no idea how to golf. While this detail might not matter, there's an equal chance it may have been beneficial for you to have prowess in the sport that your boss enjoys because it may make him more inclined to like you. In another example, imagine an inexperienced cook that believes there is only one way to make a certain dish. This is the way they have been shown and that is the only way they have ever known, so they go on believing that this dish can only be prepared in one way. This is the natural state of reality for this cook, questioning if there are any other ways to cook this dish would almost seem foolish to him because it would just be a waste of time considering such a possibility. This cook feels that he should just stick with what works. However, if this person was educated on the various possible ways of making this certain meal, new doors of opportunity would open for him. If he had ever stopped to think of other ways to make this meal, or if he would have searched for alternate preparation tactics, he could have come to new conclusions or maybe even create something revolutionary. He might have even discovered ways to cook the meal with greater celerity and zest. Overall, with his increase in cooking skills comes the increase of options at his disposal – in other words - the meals he can achieve. This is why it is important for one to constantly customize themselves, to ensure that they will be adequately equipped to create bigger and better things and continue to maximize their self-improvement. In simple terms, the more competencies you possess the more activities you are prepared for. The more we customize ourselves with various and unique insight, the more we can effectively partake in the world, hence increasing our possibility.

Education as customization is a critical aspect to realize because education enhances our personal autonomy. The customization of education allows people to explore more paths in the world and to choose the paths that most interest them. Education is an enhancing agent in our lives. As humans, we are all born with a default setting: we each have a desire to survive. It is the things we are taught, the customs we acquire, the values instilled in us by our parents, culture, and society that help mold us into the people we are at this current moment. In a sense, these things customize us before we are even able to develop our own unique way of thinking. Often, we are educated in a misguided way by our environment, but it is our own personal duty to customize ourselves in a way that will groom us to develop our full potential. There are some people that teach their children to use education in order to customize or add more variety to their arsenal. Others teach their kids to view the world in a unilateral manner and these kids unwittingly grow up believing that this truly is the only way to perceive the world. But education is not meant to provide us with one limited practical comprehension of the world. There are many ways to view and interpret the world and the things that occur inside of it. Education involves having options, be it in general or regarding whatever field of expertise you thrive in. To further illustrate the notion of education as customization, consider a car. This car is in its factory setting with generic wheels, basic body, no paint job, etc. Now let's say you just bought this car in its factory state and decide to take it to the professional mechanic to get it suped up. Maybe you will deck out the side doors, or have a spoiler installed on the back. Maybe you don't focus on outward appearances of the car, maybe you focus on the engine, the transmission, and the inner workings that affect the overall driving performance. Maybe you don't change anything and you just make sure you have all the bare necessities for the car such as gas, antifreeze, oil, etc. Regardless of how you decide to modify your ride, assuming you do anything at all, you will be improving or altering it in some way to serve a particular purpose. This particular purpose is determined by you, be it a purpose for aesthetics or driving performance. Either way you decide what it is. Hopefully, our customizations will be prudent ones. Now, instead of a car and a mechanic shop, think of a human being and education respectively. Analogous to the car going to the mechanic shop, education is the outlet in which we can improve ourselves as individuals. Similar to how you can choose to focus on certain aspects of the car that you want to improve, you can also focus on different parts of yourself as a human being. Some people choose to learn dancing or singing while others seek the facts of science, and still another person is drawn to the expressions of art. There are even people that choose to endeavor on a multitude of these avenues. Some seek to enhance their knowledge on evil or deceit. Others wish to augment their spiritual cohesion. Whatever the field of pursuit, it is something that the subject desires. It is chosen by them, provided they do not reside in a country which imposes on these natural rights of choice.

Similar to how some people don't change anything on the car at the mechanic but just buy the basic needs for the vehicle, there are people that gain a basic overall frame of reference of the world or any given field, and then they go on using their minimal practical comprehension in a limited navigation of the world. Overall, it is important to remember this aspect of education because it involves our ability to be flexible in a variety of scenarios. When things of varying nature challenge us, a well-customized individual has a better chance of dealing with the issues effectively than a person who lives a unilateral existence with a minute number of abilities or competencies.

Activity: Additional Aspects?

ShowTime!

Now it's your turn, what are some other aspects of education you would add? Why would they be considered aspects instead of essential qualities? What is their importance in regard to education?

Aspect of Education:

_____

_____

_____

_____

_____

_____

_____

_____

_____

_____

_____

_____

_____

Chapter 6

Essentials of Education

Although the aspects of education are important elements to be aware of, there are a few deeper qualities of education that need to be discussed in order to further describe what education is. So far, we have discussed what can be called "sufficient truths" of education. These are the things that happen to be a coincidental property of education, a by-product of education's root qualities. Now we will explore the necessary truths of education. Disclaimer: I am not affirming here that these are the only qualities of education; to do so would limit the possibilities that it has to offer. I believe education is an ongoing process that is constantly open to revision and improvement. Following are the qualities that I have observed so far that are intrinsic to the nature of education. If education were stripped of these qualities, it would cease to be education. I expect other educators, thinkers, and philosophers have further attributes to add to this list. These qualities are: insight exposure, learning, practical comprehension, progress, and failure. These are qualities inherent to education; they are necessary to actualize its process. We will explore each quality individually, why it is so essential to education and how it fulfills this vital role.

Insight Exposure

Insight exposure, commonly known as teaching, is the inception of education. It even precedes learning, for how can you learn something without some sort of exposure to it? The word teaching has many connotations and baggage attached to it. By uttering the word teach, many people have a predetermined idea of the word in their mind before anything has even started and they may assume to already know of what I am referring to. I do realize that teaching involves the explanation of new revelations from an exposer to a learner in a way that is palatable. However, I would implore you to suspend the common notion that implicitly comes to your mind as you think of this word. By teaching, I do not mean in reference to official schooling or only to someone that is knowingly imparting knowledge to another. Teaching is being referred to in a broader sense. Here, teaching can be conceived as the *exposure to new information*, hence why I elected the term 'insight exposure'. In his section on teaching and learning, Gert Biesta employs the words of B.P. Komisar, "…the intention of teaching might better be captured in terms of the 'awareness' of an 'auditor'…who is successfully becoming aware of the point of the act [of teaching]" (Biesta, 2017). Again, while the concept of teaching does involve explaining something to an interlocutor, I would like to add that an important part of the concept of teaching is that it makes you aware of things that exist in the world. Without being revealed to new information in the first place, how can anyone go on to learn about something of which they are not aware? Take for example, a martial art such as Wing Chun. This style relies not only on physical ability but strong mind as well. There is a deep history of the fighting style. If you never knew of the existence of this way of fighting, it is not likely that you will become a master of the art by the standard of the other masters that are invested in the same path. How would you be able to learn something of which you are not aware? Even if you stumbled upon some moves by accident without knowing they belonged to that fighting style, it would still not be assembled in a way that resembled Wing Chun. The moves would just be misplaced fractions of a whole. To further illustrate the notion of teaching as the exposure to information, it will be beneficial to explore the various types of exposure to knowledge that are present in our reality.

Real-World Experiences

This involves exposure to new knowledge by actively engaging in new experiences. When new things happen to you, they reveal new information to you, but if you aren't tuned in, you might miss the broadcast. Stated differently, how rich and deep the revelation is depends on that person's current knowledge and awareness at the moment as well as their perspective on education. Consider two individuals, Mark and James, exploring a new country for the first time. Mark is an allotted educatist and James is an engage educatist. Although they are both embarking on the same journey, they each will come away from the experience with varied levels of insight. For the allotted educatist, he may be relegating his experience of this new culture to a simple vacation to escape from everyday stress. While some people may want to explore another country for reasons similar to this one, there are also more profound reasons for this exploration and richer information that could be obtained from going abroad; one may even be able to draw parallels between a foreign culture and their own. Since Mark is used to setting aside time to learn and time to relax, it is possible for him to miss opportunities to learn during periods in which he refers to as 'relaxation time'. Since this vacation abroad qualifies as ultimate relaxing time for Mark, his mind is not oriented around learning. While he still obviously possesses the ability to learn, it is not at the forefront of his awareness during his periods reserved for pleasure. On his trip, he may learn a few words native to the country he is visiting or find out that he now has a new favorite food. He may even learn a few of their customs depending on how long he stays there. However, because his mindset was not focused on constantly learning and gaining new practical comprehension, he does not learn as much as he could have. Much of the things that he does learn while abroad are more trivial knowledge than anything insightful, provided he doesn't forget the facts shortly after gaining them. A few months after the trip, Mark is left with only an impression of his experience, how it made him feel. He has not really added on to himself as a person or gained knowledge that has changed his perspective on the world or his own existence. His gain in insight is shallow and lacks any true consequence. He is there for the enjoyment of the experience. On the contrary, if he did actually gain some knowledge that changed the way he viewed the world or was of great insight, all I advocate is that being oriented toward engage education during his adventure would have affected him in a more salient way.

However, James' experience of the trip differed from Mark's. Unlike Mark, whose main goal of going abroad was personal enjoyment, James has a deeper and more open-minded outlook of this journey. He senses the vast difference between his culture and the one of which he now visits. As he explores this new world, James stumbles upon insights into his own culture that have been made evident by experiencing another culture firsthand. This revelation is made *more* possible for James because of the stance he adopts when embarking on his trip. He is going into the experience not only aware of his surroundings, but he is also ready to find key insights in everyday occurrences. To clarify, I do not mean to imply that Mark is unable to achieve this same insight. Rather, I posit that James has a higher likelihood of noticing new insights because of the way he is engaged with the world. James is going into the trip thinking "I wonder what new things I will learn today" while Mark is going into the trip wondering "Hmm, how many enjoyable things can I do today?" There is a difference between the two sentiments. The key nuance between the engage educatist and the allotted educatist is a matter of focus. Each educatist accentuates different parts of their experience.

Real-world teaching is not structured or administered. Like air, it is readily available at any moment. It is because of this omnipresence of opportunity that one should strive for engage education; this will increase one's chances of tuning into the rewards available to those searching for them. To tune in would involve using everything that happens to you as a chance to grow. This means turning setbacks into stepping-stones to launch you further ahead. For example, if my car won't start, rather than letting frustration guide my actions I use this as a challenge activity. I simply assume the universe is providing me a chance to practice maintaining my positive attitude while focusing on finding solutions. Normally, when I wasn't oriented toward this engage education mindset, I would often not fully apply myself which led to complacency and mediocrity. In this example of the car, I would have been more likely to complain and brood about my situation long before taking any action. With engage education, I'm focused on learning lessons and seizing opportunity. Similarly, the goal in our school system ought to be helping learners to see the world through this engage outlook. It is necessary to leverage the omnipresence of real-world teaching by helping students to tune in to the opportunist viewpoint. In adopting this mindset, our children are more likely to overcome challenges, actively self-improve, and achieve personal success.

In summary, in real-world teaching, the sources of teaching are: personal experience, events, discussions, advice from others, and other things in your everyday environment. The world teacher could be in the form of a person, situation, or an intangible managing of emotions. Here, the focus is not to deliberately expose one to knowledge. Rather, the goal in natural teaching is simply to live one's life and grow stronger through experiences. The information that you learn along the way is a byproduct of living. How useful or deep that information or insight affects you is in part, reliant on your educational disposition.

Official Schooling

In the general school system, students are provided with different sources that supply them with fast access to information. Teachers, textbooks, and educational documentaries are all parts of the schooling system that are designed to expose students to new information. This type of teaching is an active effort to reveal information to students. One main tool in the utility belt of official schooling is the class curriculum. The goal of this is to provide students with a foundation of knowledge that they can refer back to. Official schooling seeks to make us aware of the achievements of other humans throughout history. This method of exposure to information is administered and regulated with a particular schedule and duration. It is an organized way to let others know about the existence of various facts, occurrences, and ways of thought. In addition to its focus on knowledge revelation, schools also limit the types of knowledge that students study as well as what is accepted as intelligence. Unfortunately, in our American society schools have turned knowledge and intelligence into commodities that further divide not only equitable access to learners but also deny their basic human rights. In a 2015 education conference at the Deming Institute, educator Alfie Kohn made the point "The school system focuses on individual and demographic short-comings as a way to distract from the systemic practices facilitating injustice" (Kohn, 2015). With the heavy focus on grades and ranking, it becomes increasingly difficult for students to learn simply for its own sake. Further in his speech Kohn states, "The student that is led to focus on solely achieving a good grade is a student who is not deeply engaged with the learning itself" (Kohn, 2015). The results of this problem in education are twofold: 1) Students do not have the time to exercise curiosity and really understand a topic and how to apply it in real life 2) Schools are not providing enough meaningful and relevant classroom content. In doing this, not only do schools prevent students from deep and creative thinking, they also deter them from wanting to participate or offer insight from their own perspective. Each student has something unique to offer, schools must recognize this truth in order to cultivate a supportive and interdependent environment. With the focus on ranking and competition, this method of "education" as it stands now seeks only to strip learners of their natural creativity and curiosity.

Self-Teaching

The next type of informational exposure to take note of is self-teaching. As the name denotes, self-teaching involves one exposing themself to new information. This method can be executed in various ways such as reading, research, studying, etc. While official schooling inculcates discipline into its students via rules and regulations, self-teaching requires the person to create and utilize their own discipline in order to be diligent in their studies. In self-teaching, you are required to have: 1) a desire to absorb new information 2) consistency in your efforts of inquiry. This method is heavily dependent on the intrinsic drive of the person.

Acquisition of Values - Cultural Teaching

This type of knowledge exposure may have the greatest effect on the development of an individual because this is the one method that has been pervading our mind since birth. I would classify this style of knowledge exposure the most active because it is constantly occurring. Each moment, an individual of a certain culture is being bombarded with messages, subtle gestures, actions, etc. that tell information about that particular culture, what is involved in it, and how they should behave inside of the culture. Educational philosopher George Counts makes a similar point to this, "Man is born helpless. He achieves freedom, as a race and as an individual, through the medium of culture. The most crucial of all circumstances conditioning human life is birth into a particular culture" (Counts, 1932). Although I am not speaking of freedom here, it is clear Counts acknowledges the profound effect that our native culture plays in influencing our life. The main focus of cultural teaching is to have individuals comport themselves in a manner that aligns with that specific culture's beliefs. This form of teaching specifically involves the youth because they are the most common ones that are absorbing new ideas and attempting to obtain a practical comprehension of the immediate world around them. When looking at cultural teaching, it is important to note that this form of revealing information is a bulk of where an individual grounds their values and belief systems. That is why this method of teaching is especially delicate, after all, the status of one's values plays a big role in shaping how they view and behave in the world. Unlike official schooling, this form of teaching is not administered; instead, it is ingrained into the individual for the duration of them living in their native culture until they move to another culture for the same process to be repeated, unless of course they create their own culture. Acquisition of values is overtly and covertly disseminated, and it is present in various aspects of life. Interestingly enough, acquisition of values actually takes on the engage education style, education as a mindset. The consistent presence of culture is what makes it so effectual. For youth aged 0-18 in particular, acquisition of values can positively or negatively affect one's outlook on education and their exposure to knowledge. For instance, if a culture prioritizes rest, relaxation, and consumption, the individuals of that culture might be less inclined to seek out knowledge. They may be accustomed to doing only what is expected of them so they can get back to their cultural comfort zone. But consider on the opposite end of the spectrum, a culture that deeply values the acquisition of new abilities and application of knowledge. It follows that members from this culture will be more likely to gain improvement. In essence, cultural upbringing exposes us to certain knowledge, beliefs, and modes of being in the world. In addition to this, it also influences the way we perceive education.

It is imperative that we do not limit our conception of what teaching is or what it involves. As we have seen, there are various types of teaching, not just the standard official schooling that is popularized. Again, these are not the only forms of insight exposure that exist, only the ones that I have written in this book. Hopefully, the exploration of these different styles aids in providing a more comprehensive view of teaching and its function in education. To reiterate, insight exposure is the inception of education. It is the attempt to explain new information to an interlocutor, and more importantly it is the initial revelation of knowledge to an individual. However, just because you expose a person to knowledge and do your best to explain the new information that is being revealed to them, it is not a guaranteed fact that the recipient will comprehend what you are exposing. It is here at this precise moment, from exposing one to information to them absorbing the information, that the learning lacuna is found. The learning lacuna is the gap that takes place between teaching and learning. It occurs when new concepts are explained to an interlocutor and these ideas are assumed to be received and understood without the learner actually learning the information. Simply stated, the learning lacuna is proof that exposure and explanation of a concept is not a guarantee that an individual will absorb and retain the new information. I posit that there are two huge factors that cause this gap to occur. The first derives from the strict requirement for teachers to teach to the test which eliminates any time for meaningful and relevant learning. Due to the limited timeframe that an insight revealer has in the classroom, they spend much of their time simply 'covering' information without diving deep into it for true understanding. Writer Matt Lynch states, "The dismal state of today's K-12 assessments is one of the biggest reasons our public schools are failing our students" (Lynch, 43). This implies that these fabled standardized tests are simply massive hindrances to the personal success of our youth. Ultimately, if a student doesn't receive a concept for the test during class time, they are either left behind or told to take extra time after class which takes away from the time they would spend doing homework, unwinding, or with family. The second derives from the fact that the very notion of learning is misconceived by many. Consequently, learning is the second component in the essential qualities of education. It is assumed to be a part of teaching, but it is its own separate process. Biesta raises questions on this idea in The Rediscovery of Teaching, "Does teaching necessarily lead to learning? Should the sole ambition of teaching be to bring about learning? Is it possible to think of teaching outside of the confines of learning?" (Biesta, p. 22). These questions are brilliant because they seek to disrupt commonly accepted notions on teaching and learning. To take this further, I posit that teaching and learning are separate occurrences because they each have their own main focus to fulfill which I will explain in a later section. In the next section, we will discuss learning, its relation to teaching, and its overall function in education.

Hey! You're still here!

Great, let's roll.

Activity: Let's Explore Insight Exposure!

What was your idea of teaching before you read this? What are your thoughts on insight exposure? With your purpose of education in mind, what are the pros and cons of viewing teaching as insight exposure?

Your Current View on Teaching:

_____

_____

_____

_____

_____

Your View on Insight Exposure:

_____

_____

_____

_____

_____

Pros	Cons

Chapter 7

Learning

So what does it mean to learn? When we learn something, we are adding that information into our personal mental to be accessed whenever we need it. When we truly learn something, it becomes a part of us. To illustrate my meaning, allow me to contrast true learning with the concept of memorizing. Memorizing is a form of temporary learning. Think back to high school when you had a big math test coming up in two days and you still couldn't tell the difference between an obtuse and acute triangle. How do you make sure you pass without using furtive tactics? You cram! You memorize the rules and the formulas well enough so that you will be able to score at least a passing grade. Not surprisingly, the day after the exam it's like you never even knew what math was! This is an exaggeration, but it is highly likely that you have forgotten most if not all of the information on the test. Why is that? Well, the information that you rapidly obtained wasn't truly learned, it was merely rented. The significance of this distinction is the transient possession of information opposed to the permanent retention of it. To restate differently, when you memorize information, you only own it for a short period of time and then it's gone. I am not referring to items in one's long-term memory for those are pieces of information that have been truly learned and infused into that person's consciousness. Here I am referencing only rented information stored in short term memory. Rented information is not incorporated into who you are as a person. However, upon truly learning something, it stays with you. It affects who you are and it makes up a portion of your cognitive arsenal; it is another piece of your unique personality. For these reasons, I refer to learning as the absorption and retention of information or knowledge. It is the act of gaining a practical comprehension of the knowledge being exposed; the information that is learned is used to help that person view and behave in the world. You can teach all you want, but if the person is not absorbing your knowledge and coming away with a practical comprehension of your information, then learning has not occurred. This is another problem in our K-12 schools. Schools tend to overlook the learning lacuna and have prioritized memory over true understanding. As an educator or parent, you probably already know why this is an issue. There is a lack of real growth for the student! They memorize things that don't matter to take tests made for a limited audience to rank against peers. But memory isn't all bad, in fact it is vital to becoming fully human. Let's explore memory in education.

Memory

So if learning is the absorption and retention of new information, what is its relation to teaching? The two are dependent on one another. Since insight exposure is the inception of education, it serves as the foundation of learning. If teaching is the exposure and explanation of new concepts, then learning is the acquisition and retention of these concepts. Therefore, where teaching ends, learning begins. So what facilitates the learning process? One obvious facet of this is physical health and capability. One's mental faculties must be fully operational and be able to store information for future use. While memorizing is a way of renting information, the process of *remembering* is a crucial element to learning. For learning, memory is the adhesive that holds all the knowledge that you've accumulated over time. For without memory, you could not build a foundation to begin with! For this reason, it is crucial to note the significance of memory in the learning process. Take for example you are learning a new language. In a language, you usually learn rudimentary vocabulary words and some of the basic grammar rules. However, if you are unable to remember and internalize the rules of the language or the basic vocabulary, you will not be able to reach fluency. How can you make these words and rules a part of your repertoire if you forget them every time you go to retrieve them in your mind? It would be hard for you to try to use your Spanish skills to ask for the price of a book if you could never remember how to say the proper phrases. Hence, memory provides you access to information that you have obtained. But just because the information is accessible does not mean that you automatically remember everything that you encounter. For you to recall information that you choose to retain, you must be *present* when learning. Moreover, while memory is certainly important, schools have become fixated with this part of the education process. To inspire creativity and ingenuity, we must provide students with various ways of engaging as a learner with multiple manners of displaying their intelligence.

Focus and Desire

     To stimulate this discussion, it would be beneficial to begin with some questions. First, let's ponder the idea of desire and learning. Is desire *required* to learn? Better still, consider the question: can you learn even if you do not want to? Is it possible to learn by mistake? To answer these odd questions, let's imagine a young adult college graduate that is looking to pursue their Master's. In order to be admitted to graduate school, there are various requirements that this student must meet. Of these requirements is a standardized test known as the GRE. This test consists of verbal, math, and writing exercises. Unless you enjoy standardized testing, this is a tedious part of the application process. But alas, this is what is required in order to be admitted into a graduate program. So our hypothetical student must prepare for it. Now even though our prospective graduate student doesn't *want* to be bothered with the testing information, he is still able to access a teaching method and he can absorb knowledge on the appropriate subjects. Here, it is clear that the student doesn't have the desire to participate with the GRE material, but he is still capable of gaining knowledge to earn a decent score. Whether or not he retains the information afterward is inconclusive. It is likely that because of his disregard for the GRE, his learning will probably only be temporary at best. So what enables him to learn new information despite his own wishes? Well, one might say that his desire to attend graduate school outweighed his desire to disregard the GRE and therefore desire is the active agent for his behavior. And this would be a fair assessment; desire as the motivating factor of learning usually leads to effectual retention. Simply put, desire is the fuel for one's learning. So, the focus for learners is to truly intend to gain insight for the betterment of themselves and to achieve their life purpose. They should not be coerced to learn something because it was imposed upon them by limited standardized practices. This is not to imply that an individual will always have to like every part of the learning process. Some parts are challenging and it is this very reason that the student must endure, for nothing exceptional comes via an easy path. The interesting question for the insight revealer here is how to create a class climate and culture in which learning is viewed as necessary and vital to one's success, development, and human cultivation. One way that I strive to create a climate where learners are engaged is by using examples, topics, songs, and activities that are relevant to them. For example, I recently did a seminar on stress management with my 8th graders. We were talking about creating personal mantras or positive affirmations that help to create your own mental weather. As a bridge, I asked them, "What do you think the rapper Cardi B tells herself?" As you can imagine, there was some surprise at the mention of a rapper in class but then almost immediately the kids told me, "She says, 'I'm a boss bitch!' " If you are wondering, no we didn't say the explicit version! Then I asked them, "Okay so how do you think that makes her feel?"

Many of them responded with things like, confidence, strong, and empowered. Although this may be unorthodox, the point is that I was able to use that as an example of an affirmation that provides personal confidence, which many of them agreed this phrase equaled in some fashion. If you want to make a real connection and show your students you are human, take the time to study up on what is current, trending, and important to your class demographic. What shows, songs, or activities interest them? To help find some of these answers, simply ask your students one of these questions and have them anonymously write their response on a piece of paper. Collect it and boom you've got data! Most importantly, ensure that whichever tactic you use to build a bridge with your students - be it a joke, anecdote, or relevant example - is coming off genuinely and authentically. If you are artificial in your delivery or try to force it, your learners will sense it immediately and may be offput.

After possessing adequate desire, the act of learning is then facilitated by another factor which I will refer to as focus. This is the second aspect that vitalizes the learning process. So why is focus important in relation to learning? Returning to our future graduate student, let's think of a GRE study session in which he pays limited attention to the information being exposed and explained. We can imagine this in two teaching methods. First, picture our graduate student using a self-teaching style to expose himself to GRE strategies and tactics. During this session while watching clips on how to successfully answer text completion questions he is also talking to his girlfriend on the phone. At this moment, his focus is split between two activities: learning verbal techniques and talking to his girlfriend. It is not hard to imagine that this behavior will lower his retention of both activities. Additionally, consider the same student is signed up for a GRE study group administered by a tutor. The tutor is lecturing on geometry concepts and while this lecture is occurring, our graduate student is lost in thoughts of his plans for the weekend; despite the teacher exposing and explaining new information to him, his lack of focus results in him learning little to nothing at all. Likewise, in the instance with his self-study and his girlfriend, due to his split attention his capacity to learn GRE concepts in that moment is mitigated. Therefore, it stands to reason that focus is an important factor that should be present in order to learn more effectively. This isn't a new message; however, I do want to emphasize the true power of focus. Sales training CEO Grant Cardone talks about focus in his concept of four degrees of action. In his 10x Rule he explains, "…although each level varies in potency, all the degrees of action require pretty much the same amount of focus and energy. The ability to shift one's focus from distracting and destructive items to practices that will foster their success is a simple one" (Cardone, 2011). However, simple doesn't imply easy. Hence, the challenge here is how can we help students to use the power of focus and paradigm shifting to their advantage? My immediate response to this question would be to help learners to set respectable goals for themselves that are just out of their reach. In helping students to find their 'why' or their reason for striving for success, it is more likely for them to exhibit increased focus provided the goals are relevant to them. Quick note on this, while this can be applied to school and grades, it is far more important to teach S.M.A.R.T. goals in terms of life purpose and daily actions. To be frank, often times when students are disengaged it is because they do not see the point in paying attention. For this reason, educators must ensure that they are helping their students to set S.M.A.R.T. goals that are a bit of a challenge to achieve. [2] In doing this, learners will

---

[2] S.M.A.R.T. stands for Specific, Measurable, Achievable, Relevant, and Timely. It is a great method for setting solid goals and actively tracking progress toward those goals.

be more inclined to stay on task because: 1) they are working on something of interest 2) they have the ability to track their progress in real-time, which can help in gamifying the process 3) they are pushing pass their limits. Most importantly, in setting their own personal goals they will be working toward something that is relevant to them, not something chosen for them.

*For more on how to inspire desire and focus within learners, see the activity at the end of this chapter entitled: Applying What We Learn (p.62). This is originally meant for educators, but this can be easily adapted for your learners. This will inspire focus and desire within them because they will get to choose what they learn and apply. *

Ultimately, even if you are exposed to knowledge that is explained in a cogent way, you must also be tuned into the message or you will not receive it. As educators, it is our task to help student's shift their focus from allotted education to engage education. Once we can facilitate this paradigm shift, we will see learners begin to thrive and flourish at faster rates. Education is a non-stop process, if we cannot help learners to be constantly tuned into the exposure of new concepts, all they will hear in response from the world is static. How do we help them to be tuned in? By including learners into the development process of class climate, school policies, and curriculum design. It is imperative that we actively make learners feel like they belong and play an important role in the education process. In addition, we must truly value student voice and opinion. No longer can we relegate the youth to underdeveloped adults, for they are people in their own right. They have things to reveal to us, just as we do for them. Instead of holding them up to the standards of adults, we need to accept children for who they are in their current state. Only then can we truly begin to learn with and from them, as we want them to do for us. If students feel like they are active agents in schooling instead of mere subjects to it, they would certainly be more genuinely excited to come and contribute to the school community.

To gain a more detailed view of what learning includes, it is wise to explore the various types of learning. Although there are certain to be others, there are three general types of learning that will be discussed. These types are sense, vicarious, and praxis.

Sense Learning

Using our senses to gain intelligence about the world around us is a staple method of acquiring knowledge known as empiricism. This style of learning is an integral part of the human experience. Sense learning is a foundation needed to actualize our perception of reality; if sense learning did not exist, our experience of the world would be ineffable. With this method, we first must observe the world and the information being displayed to us via the usage of our senses. Once this observation is complete, we digest the information and use that data in reference to something else. For example, when we experience the notion of extreme heat. We don't just observe heat and take it alone as an arbitrary piece of information. In contrast, it is meaningful to us in a number of particular ways. Think of astronauts needing extreme temperatures and combustion force to send space aircrafts into Earth's orbit. Or with lesser fires, think of bakers that require their oven in order to create entrees for their customers. When we learn about fire and how it can benefit us, it now has a value to us. That's why people pay for firewood, something that is available for free if you were willing to go and axe a tree on your own time. Now when we take this notion of heat in physical relation to ourselves, we find that it is hot and painful to the touch. In an optical sense, we see that it is a bright orange hue, and that it is always in motion. We can hear the cackle of flames or the whoosh of a fire blast. The scent of fire individually is elusive, however whatever material it is consuming has a distinct odor. All the things that we learn from fire are via our senses. From this it follows that without our senses, it is not possible to retain or absorb any details from our experience. The retention of this information aids in creating a frame of reference for the learner. However, despite the importance of the senses in the actualization of learning - and our awareness of the world - the senses can also mislead the learner and sometimes cause them to store inaccurate information in their minds similar to Descartes' example of the stick in the water. In the meditations Descartes talks about this very topic, and his example is the bent perception of the stick when viewed by an observer standing outside the body of water. [3] Similarly, remember that social blunder when you thought you saw your friend or your co-worker, only to later realize they were someone else? Yes, totally embarrassing I know!

Since sense learning involves gaining information in reference to something else, it follows that this method of learning deals with drawing connections between what is perceived and the ideas attributed to the given phenomenon.

Drawing Connections

The first point here is the role of direct experience. Suppose, prior to your knowledge of what a house looks like, you are only told via words on what a house is. You are informed of its various functions including sleep, shelter, food, and hygiene. If you can absorb and retain this information on a house, can you say that you learned what a house is? Despite not

---

[3] See Meditation One in *Meditations* - Descartes was huge on distrusting the senses and wanted to ascertain foundational truths about the world. Hence it is vital we ensure our frame of references are correct before acting on them.

having a personal experience of the house or seeing its appearance, can you truly understand a house based on theory alone? Well, if you say that learning is the absorption and retention of information, then yes you can say you learned theoretically *about* the house. But this knowledge of the house is still inchoate. Although you have learned about what a house is and of its function, you still have no visual representation or any immediate personal experience of the house. Your understanding of the house is incomplete if you have never been in it and only possess a theoretical awareness of it. You have nothing to relate back to it and therefore you have an imperfect comprehension of it. It doesn't truly resonate with you. In Biesta's terms, "…I zoom in on the idea of the learner, asking what, in common understandings of learning, it actually means to exist as a learner…I particularly focus on the idea that learning is to be understood as an act of sense-making or comprehension." (Biesta, 23). Going back to our example of the house, it follows that as a learner you cannot truly 'make-sense' of it as Biesta says. To make our understanding of a house more detailed, it would be beneficial to learn not only it's functions but also to receive a visual depiction of it. To go a step further, your knowledge of the house would be even stronger if you were standing inside of one. What's more, if you began to live in that house, you would begin to further your knowledge on what it entails. Simply put, there are varying degrees to which one can know something. But let's take a few steps back to when you never seen a house in person before and only learned about it theoretically. It is important to learn about the functions as well as the visuals of the house because this is how drawing connections works. If you've never known or experienced a house before and you are told of its functions, you would now want to see it in action. After learning about the house, it would help to see pictures of its physical appearance. This aids in the process of drawing connections between the depiction of the house and its various functions and qualities. Now, whenever you do see the house in your experience, you will be able to relate those learned ideas back to its appearance. This process of drawing connections between ideas in our mind and sense data in the outside world is what helps concretize understanding and allows us to gain practical comprehension of anything.

A further component of drawing connections is comparing new information with items already known. This aids in the retention of new concepts. Take for instance, you have strong knowledge on what a house is, and now you are learning about a cabin. You are exposed to the description of the cabin and you are told of its function. You hear that the cabin is an area for you to sleep in, eat meals, and take care of hygiene. Almost automatically, you begin equating the idea of a cabin to that of a house. Why? Relating new ideas to already known ones makes it easier to retain the new knowledge. Hence, the importance of drawing connections in relation to sense learning is the fact that these mental links aid in grasping new concepts. To further illustrate this notion, consider what is involved with augmenting one's vocabulary. When you first hear an advanced word such as erudite, you are unsure of its meaning. Unless you can deduce its definition through contextual clues, it makes no sense to you. It has no significance or relevance to you in any way. This irrelevance and displacement are so apparent because you have never experienced the word before. In order to gain some modicum of comprehension, you ask the user of the word to use it again in a different sentence. This tactic is good because it helps to provide that context that you are hunting for. If this method is unsuccessful, you could also ask the person to give you synonyms for that word. You ask this question in hopes that you will recognize one of the words in the enumeration so that you will have an idea to anchor to the unknown word. This is a prime instance of drawing connections because it relies on current knowledge as a frame of reference for attaining new information. By making a connection between a known word and a new word, we are able to gain a practical comprehension of that word and add it into our vocabulary. Drawing connections between words that are similar allows you to learn more effectively as opposed to simply hearing the definition of the word alone. Provided you know the synonyms of the new word, they will give experiences to it, not just ideas. Again, if you were verbally told the meaning of erudite you may or may not understand it, but it is less likely that you will retain the meaning. In contrast, it is more likely for you to remember the meaning if you linked the new word to a known word in your vocab-cache. Upon exposure to the word erudite, it would be helpful to pair its definition to other words such as 'smart' and 'intelligent' because this will allow you to add another name to the same idea of which you are already familiar. These basic words serve as a bridge between your current knowledge and the new knowledge you have acquired. Conclusively, this shows that drawing connections between current knowledge and new information helps to retain and solidify details into one's mind as knowledge they own, not rent.

Vicarious Learning

The next style is termed vicarious learning, also referred to as learning via observation. This form of learning occurs simply by watching others perform an action and replicating their movements. To clarify, this is limited to the individual's physical or mental ability level. Think of you trying to reproduce a perfect split - without injury to your body - if you aren't flexible; it will not be the same as the perfect sample that you perceived. Through watching others, we can gain information from their experience and use those details to help guide our own endeavors. Like sense learning, this method has its pros and cons. On one hand, this method of learning is helpful because it is a simple duplication process. The learner observes an action, absorbs the steps involved in that action, and then reproduces it themselves. This process is quick and direct. However, trouble arises when the actions become more complex. In other words, it is probably easier to vicariously learn to ride a skateboard than it is to learn a tumble routine in gymnastics. While observational learning is a good tool to acquire knowledge, it lacks the involvement aspect that is absolutely necessary in learning. In order to learn more effectively, it is prudent to be actively engaged with the information that one is learning. This is in line with Dewey's idea of learning by doing, "It is essentially the ability to learn from experience; the power to retain from one experience something which is of avail in coping with the difficulties of a later situation. This means power to modify actions on the basis of the results of prior experiences, the power to develop dispositions" (Dewey, 1916). If the child was not directly engaged in an activity themselves, it makes it harder for them to retain the exposed intel. In addition, if they aren't actively making their own experiences, then they will be unable to develop their own frame of reference or 'disposition' to use Dewey's term. Thus, this active participation triggers your mind differently as opposed to if you were just listening to new information. When you are directly involved with the new information being presented to you, you are making more connections and in turn, further fortifying your retention contrary to simply watching or hearing the information. For an illustration of this, see Edgar Dale's cone of learning in Figure 1 (Dale, 1946):

After 2 weeks, we tend to remember...		Involvement
10% of what we READ	Reading	P A S S I V E
20% of what we HEAR	Hearing Words	
30% of what we SEE	Seeing	
50% of what we SEE & HEAR	Watching a Movie Looking at an Exhibit Watching a Demonstration Seeing It Done on Location	
70% of what we SAY	Participation in a Discussion Giving a Talk	A C T I V E
90% of what we DO	Doing a Dramatic Presentation Simulating the Real Experience Doing the Real Thing	

Figure 1

In the depiction, the retention rate correlates to the way in which we are engaged in the exposure and absorption of information. In other words, we remember more of what we actually DO as opposed to what we merely read or see.

Consider driving as an example of this. Think of when you are in a driving class listening to an instructor talk about a specific detail like looking over your left shoulder when you are merging left. This kind of advice tends to elude you because it has no true resonance with you, no meaning. It doesn't relate to you in any particular way because you have no experience of it. Only when you are out on the road and you begin to make your merge into the left lane and are met with an abrupt blaring of the driver that recently appeared in your blind spot is when this advice is applicable to you. In another example, verbally telling someone - without any visual aid - how to throw a baseball may yield the desired result. However, showing them how to do it with an actual ball and helping them in the process of throwing it correctly will yield stronger results. Ben Franklin is believed to have said, "Tell me, I will forget. Show me and I may remember. But involve me and I will understand." Whether or not it was he who uttered these words is irrelevant, it is the message that is crucial. The main point to note here is that educators MUST get kids *involved*. Only then will our efforts promote stronger learning and development. An interesting point about vicarious learning is that it implicitly involves insight revealers, some of which who are not even aware that they are showing someone else how to do something! This is due to the fact that the focus is not really on the exposers, but on the observer. In vicarious learning, the learner's attention is what actualizes this learning method. Moreover, there are parallels between self-teaching and vicarious learning. In self-teaching, the responsibility is on the person exposing themselves to knowledge, no one does it for them. Similarly in vicarious learning, the responsibility is reserved only for the learner to gain the knowledge being displayed. The major difference between the former and the latter is the origin of the information. In self-teaching you utilize multiple sources to gain knowledge. In vicarious learning, the main source of knowledge acquisition is the behavior of others. The concepts of vicarious learning and self-teaching are related because they both require the exact same thing of the learner: to have an *active will* to gain new knowledge, not just attention but an advancing agenda, a hunting mindset to salvage knowledge at their own discretion. In vicarious learning, a potential lesson could go completely unnoticed if a learner is not oriented toward the lesson. To vitalize this concept, imagine you are in the woods on a hiking trail. On your journey, you enter a clearing and you pass by a family assembling a tent. They seem like experienced camp enthusiasts and they are making good progress with their project. Here, there is a potential opportunity to learn vicariously. You could choose to stick around for a while and politely ask to observe the process so that you could learn from their experience. However, because you have no desire to learn details on tent erection, you simply continue through the clearing and progress on your hiking trail. In this instance, the possibility of learning through observation was available, but since the hiker had no active will to learn about setting up tents, he paid no attention to the process and decided to continue walking on his journey. This idea can be applied to more esoteric and abstract insights as well. There are many things in this world in terms of spirituality, intrapersonal knowledge, intuition, and interdependence that we as humans regularly fail to tap into. From this it follows that observational learning requires both the attention and the active will of the learner in order to be executed. There could be a plethora of potential lessons being revealed to an individual on a daily basis, but if the person has no need or desire to learn that given thing, it is less likely that they will pay attention to something that they weren't searching for.

In addition to active will, attention, and replicating the actions of others, this type of learning involves learning from the mistakes of others. Often, we use others as an example or a role model to follow. However, in watching others long enough, we will inevitably watch them fail. This failure can be instructive because it can admonish us of which pathways to eschew. By learning from the mistakes of others, we expedite our own process of development by preemptively avoiding mistakes that we would have made had we not been informed vicariously.

While learning from the mistakes of others is necessary, I want to briefly highlight the importance of experiencing failure firsthand.

In some instances, for us to have a true practical comprehension of something we must experience it for ourselves. There may be some points when observing the mistake of another is not a strong reason for us to avoid the same action because we cannot know how we would behave under the same circumstances. Consider a simple example such as two young girls learning to jump double dutch. In this activity, the ropes are to be turned and then the person must time their jump correctly so they will not disturb the moving rope while jumping in time with it as many times as possible. Let's say the first child, Jill, attempts to jump into the dual ropes but her timing is off and she falters. She attempts again and again for a total of 14 tries. Finally, on her last attempt she is able to land the correct timing and jumped a total of 5 times. After this success, she informs the second girl, Amy, of things that she believes may prove helpful in landing the correct timing. Although Amy received this information from Jill, she still lacks the confidence to jump inside. This could be due to seeing Jill fail so many times at first which may be discouraging, or it could be that the ropes appear too fast to jump into. Despite the reason, hearing Jill's advice coupled with repeated failures was not enough for her to learn vicariously. Although the advice helps, Amy still fails numerous times before figuring out the timing to the double dutch ropes. Thus, for Amy to succeed, it was necessary for her to fail. Only then can she begin to progress. This is given the fact that timing is hard to explain; timing is a type of syncing of your senses. It requires deep focus and a form of visualization. It isn't taught directly via instruction but it is instilled over time. Just think of a martial artist choosing the exact moment to strike, weave, or parry an opponent. Or picture a baseball player waiting for the precise time to swing the bat in order to earn a good hit. Due to its scrupulous nature, timing is something that must be learned through trial and error.

Trial, Error and Praxis

This notion of learning from failure is a transition to the next method of learning known as trial and error. Trial and error can also be termed 'absorbing from experience'. This style of learning is an axiomatic tactic in the skillset of humanity. The process of trial and error involves doing something, failing, and eliminating that method while searching for new ones. This process is useful but can be time consuming depending on the available possibilities.

Absorbing from experience is related to another type of learning called praxis which refers to theory in practice. A notable feature of these two learning methods is that they both require a practical 'hands-on' approach from the learner. In each instance, you are actively doing something to receive feedback. In particular, the learner is in the driver's seat and they are engaged with the concepts that are being revealed to them from either method. In praxis, the person is actually using the theories and concepts exposed and it is through praxis that this learner will create a personal context from which to deduce what they are experiencing. For this reason, praxis is more effective than vicarious learning because the latter is more passive while the former actively involves the learner. To illustrate this point, consider two individuals looking to get their license. One uses observational learning to attempt the goal while the other uses praxis. The vicarious learner takes the written permit test, watches some tutorial driving videos and takes notes when in his driving class. Along with this, he frequently observes his mother and her driving style. Confident in his skills as a student, he believes that he can manage to past the driving exam based solely on his theoretical knowledge, with no actual driving lessons. At the road test, he begins to drive for the first time and he finds that theoretical driving is not synonymous with firsthand experience. Even though he knows in theory what he is supposed to do, the physical sensations of his duties are foreign to him. His spatial intelligence in reference to cars is immature and his judgement of traffic and the speed of other cars is novice. In theory, he knows how to parallel park perfectly. However, when it comes time to actualize his theoretical knowledge, he cannot help but fumble through the motions. Not surprisingly, this student fails the exam and would need to come back after some *praxis*. From examples like this we can deduce that observational learning is advantageous in familiarizing one with concepts of a given field. However, if that person stays in the theoretical aspect of that field without gaining practical experience, that person's practical comprehension of the field will be incomplete. Take on the opposite side of the spectrum, the student that had a few theoretical classes and 10 practical driving lessons. This student would be more prepared for the exam because he has personal experience of driving to draw from and he is already familiarized with the physical sensation of operating a vehicle. Consistent praxis allows one to gain an applied comprehension of the concepts. In addition, constant praxis in a given area could yield further insight in that field, insight that may not be accessible to a solely theoretical learner or a periodic praxis learner. For example, consider the act of cooking. This can be an expressive art form or it can be a simple means to an end. For the person that is making a meal to survive, they may be more inclined to cook what is quickest and most convenient. However, the professional chef has access to many more dishes because of the deeper level of praxis that he puts into the activity. The chef knows the combinations, what complements each other. He knows ways to prepare the same dish that our periodic cook can make, but with more potent taste, celerity, and accuracy. He knows the delicate details such as how long to let something grill for, or what seasoning would work best depending on the protein, or how to chop vegetables with maximum efficiency. All of these particular hints of knowledge are certainly locked off to a person that occasionally uses a recipe to cook as their only means of meal preparation; they do not have the same art and expression as the cook with his heightened practical comprehension of the culinary arts. Overall, in order to maximize one's absorption and retention of information, it is beneficial to use observational learning in conjunction with praxis. In this amalgamation, the emphasis should be on praxis because it is through active involvement that enhances one's retention of new concepts. Unfortunately, our K-12 school system focuses heavily on theory with not enough attention on praxis and application. The solution? Placing more emphasis on learning by doing!

*To jumpstart this process, see activities listed at the end of Chapter 7 and 8 *

The Key Difference between Teaching and Learning

As stated in a previous section, where teaching ends, learning begins. When a learner fails to absorb something exposed by an insight revealer it results in what I refer to as the learning lacuna. This gap between insight revelation and learning exists because of the key differences among the two. In teaching, all the things that are revealed to you originate from a source outside of yourself. In effect, this means that you *rely* on the world for knowledge. Any information that is exposed or explained to you never originates from yourself as the sole author. Even when engaged in self-teaching; although an individual is making themselves aware of knowledge, this does not mean they have learned it nor has it come directly from them as the catalyst. In other words, for you to be able to know about the existence of China, you would have to be shown it from a source in your environment i.e. your television, a verbal message from someone, or reading it in a newspaper. You could not search inside of yourself for a fact you do not know. On the opposite end, learning requires one's personal agency. While outside agents are responsible for revealing information to you, you are responsible for absorbing and retaining the information that is revealed by displaying active will and attention. Therefore, learning occurs within yourself; although someone may really want you to know something, you must actualize the process alone. In order for insight revelation and learning to work together in harmony, they must both focus on specific qualities: active involvement, hunting will and focus.

Activity: Applying What We Learn

One of the main problems in our school system is the absence of applying what we learn. If we want students to be able to directly apply information they learned to their daily lives, it is important for us to practice this ourselves. So educators, I have a challenge for you! I want you to make a list below of 4 new things that you want to learn and actively practice for the next month. It can be professional development skills, personal development, interpersonal, financial, etc. Whatever it is, make a list of these four items below. Now, for each week, I want you to focus on one of the new items, and I mean hyper focus. For instance, one of the new things that I am learning from my study of sales is that it is crucial to agree first before trying to close a prospect. To ensure I learn this concept fully, I have begun an agreement challenge where I try to genuinely find some type of agreement with each person I interact with. I try to gamify it by adding fun goals for myself, it goes like this: 1) Monday – Agree with 5 people today, no matter how outlandish their comment or how much I don't personally agree, agree that they are experiencing reality in their own unique way. 2) Tuesday – Along with each agreement, be sure to give a genuine smile and try to have the other person agree with you as well 3) Wednesday – Agree using a relatable bridge story and include empathy in your approach and try to make the other person laugh.

You can continue up until the last day of the week and then move on to your next item of practice. This activity is simple yet effective, but it will only benefit those that are serious about improving themselves so that they can better provide for others. Be sure to set a new item for each week. Also, if you feel like a week is not enough time for you to hone a concept, then by all means stay on that item until you feel comfortable doing it in practice. The point of this activity is to become more accustomed to creating opportunities to use what we learn right away.

Note: This activity can be adapted for use with your learners as well. Simply use the chart below and have them follow the same instructions that are laid out while you act as a facilitator.

I will plug my example in to the chart to get you started. I have completed up until Wednesday just so you can get an idea of how this works.

4 New Items to Learn and Apply

1. Agree then Close

2.

3.

4.

Weekdays	Fun Goal	Challenge 1	Challenge 2
Monday	Get 5 Smiles	Agree with at least 3 people, no matter how outlandish their comment. Agree that they are experiencing their reality	Find something positive to say about their opinion
Tuesday	Make 3 People Laugh	Agree with at least 5 people today, no matter the comment. Agree that they are experiencing their reality	In your interactions, be sure to let people completely finish their thoughts before you begin speaking.
Wednesday	Give out 5 genuine compliments	Agree with 7 people no matter what the comment. Agree that they are experiencing their reality	When you agree with someone today, be sure to show them that you are genuine by adding an empathetic anecdote
Thursday			
Friday			
Saturday			
Sunday			

Now it's your turn! Make a list of all the items that you would like to start implementing right away. Then set up a weekly, biweekly, or monthly challenge for yourself. Remember, the only way for your knowledge to truly benefit others is if you use it.

Chapter 8

Active Involvement, Hunting Will, and Focus

Some knowledge exposure methods like vicarious learning and official schooling tend to impart knowledge without further clarification. In the official schooling model, this is manifested in the form of lecture-style classrooms. This is also present in authoritarian households. This dynamic of exposing and explaining is a crucial contributor to the learning lacuna because it treats the transfer of knowledge as a one-way conversation in which the speaker 'knows it all' and the learner must simply accept what they say as truth. This relationship contains little active involvement between both parties because there is an underlying sense that there is only one way of doing things. Furthermore, there is little room for practical activities or discussions that could help further explicate concepts that were exposed. This process does not promote critical thinkers but only passive drones that simply accept information they hear in the world as truth.

So what bridges this gap between the sending of knowledge from an exposer of information, to the receiving and retaining of the learner? In order to make this revealer-learner relationship more seamless and beneficial to both parties, it is wise for revealers to focus on actively engaging the learners in the information. Learners cannot feel so removed from the concepts. In utilizing a more inclusive and hands-on approach by having learners engage with the information they are being exposed to, learners may be more inclined to critically think and create new avenues of thought. Furthermore, if learners feel like they were a part of the teaching process instead of a subject to it, it may increase their will to absorb the information. In addition to getting students engaged, it is necessary for insight revealers to combine their powers in an organized fashion to support an interdependent environment both in and out of the classroom. This is similar to George Counts' idea of teacher organization in the school and community. [4] However, it is not only up to teachers to bring about salient and meaningful change oriented toward humanity and organic intelligence. It is up to each and every sector of our society to work together while focusing on their own unique roles. If we can attack injustice, ignorance, and negative social programming from multiple angles at once, it will have a much greater effect. This involves parents, school administrators, policy makers, eduprenuers, teachers, students, and all other people that hold a stake in the education - not schooling - of our youth.[5] Overall to be more effective, teaching should emphasize active involvement in ways that will allow the learner to conduct immediate praxis of what is being exposed or explained while promoting a supportive and interdependent class climate.

Where teaching should be responsible for the active involvement of the learner, learning requires one to possess a hunting will and focus. A hunting will is a desire that one not only wants, but will strive for relentlessly until they have satisfied that desire. By focus I simply mean centering one's full and utter abilities on a singular task at hand. These two qualities are the implements necessary to gain and retain new information. A hunting will is required because it is what drives that person to act; it is the motivation, the fuel, the catalyst for action. Without that catalyst, it is less likely that one will even spend attention on a given task for very long because put simply, it is inconsequential to them. Once the hunting will is present, the focus must be complete and undivided. As seen in

---

[4] See p. xi of (Counts, 1932) preface section by Urban
[5] Eduprenuer here refers to an educator providing services as an entrepreneur instead of as a salary worker

the previous example with the GRE student, conducting multiple activities at once is ineffectual because it causes you to split yourself in different directions therefore severing effectiveness. Only once you are fully focused with a drive to learn is when you will be able to actualize the learning process.

Conclusively, teaching and learning requires the complete devotion of these above-mentioned attributes to their respective areas. This course of action will help to bridge the gap that occurs in the delivery of information to the reception of it. The goal should be to make teaching and learning focus on their respective duties and to minimize the amount of information that evades the learner due to poor levels of inclusion. Finally, the overall function of learning in education is to absorb and retain information to supply one's implements to be used in their path to improvement.

Activity: The Red Light Praxis

As we have discussed, schools spend a plethora of time and resources ensuring that learners know a lot of information. More specifically, schools value the student that can memorize and regurgitate information back. Since Humanization and Organic Intelligence (HOI) – discussed in chapter 12, is centered on creatively synergizing our knowledge and directly applying it, this activity will exercise your ability to help your learners apply what they have learned. Similar to the previous activity, you will be practicing applying new knowledge but this time you will be doing this as a collective class activity.

Prompt

Reserve a class period for this activity. Let's say you have 21 kids with a 56-minute period. Start at the top of the class by presenting the students with 3 new skills to learn. These skills must be something universally applicable to humanity i.e. public speaking skills, emotional intelligence, spiritual cohesion etc. Give the students 2 min to commit to a skill, and then group the students according to selected skill. For example, you have a public speaking group, emotional intelligence group, and spiritual cohesion group. They have 20 min to research the topic, 3 min each group to teach back the topic to the class so 9 min total, and 25 min to practice role-playing scenarios where they practice using the new skill right away. The last part of the exercise is most important because it is through firsthand experience that we retain information most effectively. If these times frames do not work for you, please feel free to tailor this activity to you and your student's needs.

Chapter 9

Education as Practical Comprehension

I know I have been using this phrase quite a bit since the start of this book. Through context clues, you may have already inferred the meaning of this term, however I would like to discuss this in more detail as I believe this is an essential quality of education. Practical comprehension involves knowing something and how to relate or interact with that thing. This way of interacting is usually for an intended purpose. This aspect of education is crucial because it is what enables us to navigate our daily lives. This notion of practical comprehension can be conceived with virtually anything. Consider the act of brushing your teeth. You know how to bare your teeth, rotate the toothbrush in a circular motion, and scrub the germs away. You know that in order to get in between the teeth, you need to hold your toothbrush in a specific manner. You are aware that you must also scrub your tongue when ending your tooth brushing session. This can be vividly applied to a plethora of things such as driving, playing a sport, doing math, or using a critical thinking process. A practical comprehension of something means you know how to use or engage with it in order to achieve a desired result. Once you learn how to do something, you have gained a practical comprehension of it; it is the direct application of something you have learned, no matter its complexity. One key takeaway for educators here? We must learn to help students devise creative ways of combining known items with new items. Additionally, students must be able to draw unique conclusions and new solutions. For example, let's say a student has accumulated knowledge about emotional intelligence, interpersonal communication, and marketing. With this knowledge, there is plenty of possibility at this student's disposal, however given their previous lecture-style classes their knowledge is more theory than practice so they are unsure on how to apply what they know. How can we help this student put their skills to meaningful and relevant use? Well, let's consider that our student is very interested in social media and art design. Considering student voice and interest, let's say you and your learner co-create an assignment in which the student has to create a social media campaign on Instagram to draw awareness to a hypothetical art convention. Though this student never took a course on social media marketing, using their previous knowledge of people and communication the student has a prime opportunity to exercise their knowledge to achieve a new goal. In order to create fun and relatable posts that people will engage with on Instagram, the student would have to combine their knowledge in such a way that would enable them to reach their target audience. The main point here is twofold: 1) The dire need to directly practice learned items. 2) The necessity to practice creatively combining what we know in unique ways to discover fresh solutions.

Without the praxis of what we learn, we would only be in a constant state of theorizing. Using our practical comprehension of learned information in order to fulfill a given purpose is an important quality of education that is often overlooked by our school system. To be clear, subjects such as global history, chemistry, and calculus do have some value. However, how often will students actually engage with these items on a daily basis? How often will they actually need to apply the information from the French revolution, a double-bond solution experiment, or determine the use of some advanced formula? I ask the question: if a topic or subject cannot be immediately and directly useful to a learner's life, should we even teach it? Would it not be more useful to learn about items such as emotional intelligence, active listening, or facing your fears? These are items that children will be actively engaged with on a daily basis. The main takeaway here is that mainstream schooling ought to focus on helping learners to APPLY what they learn. In conjunction, it is more likely for learners to be inclined to use information from school if it pertained to their daily experience and offered instant benefits. It is this practical application of our education that sets the foundations for new discoveries, ways of thought, and improved methods of action. In other words, if you never learn how to play tennis, how can you ever hope to improve at it? You must obtain a practical comprehension of the sport first. Consider riding a BMX bike. Gaining the balance and coordination is necessary to being able to ride the bike and this comes before you can even attempt to pop a wheelie. You must build a foundation of being able to consistently ride the bike without falling before you can perform any tricks. Once you can ride the bike without any effort, you have gained a practical comprehension of how to ride. Note, practical comprehension is not simply being intellectually aware of the concepts involved with an activity. This means that just knowing conceptually about what one needs to do in order to ride a bike is not the same as having the physical experience of riding the bike. As a result the person with the theoretical knowledge, and no physical experience, is less qualified to teach another how to ride a bike as opposed to someone that rides every day. Upon attaining practical comprehension of bike riding, the foundation for tricks has been laid. This means that you can gain a greater practical comprehension on how to use the bike for your purposes. For example, it is now possible for you to do a bunny hop or pop a wheelie because you won't have to worry so much about maintaining your speed and balance. Another example to illustrate the importance of this notion is language. Before being able to write a song, speech, or poem, you must first gain a practical comprehension of the language. You must be aware of the rules and the grammar, and how to use them appropriately. You will need vocabulary, knowledge of abstract expressions, and much more if you want to be a proficient speaker of a language. One major issue with mainstream schooling is the lack of focus on practical comprehension. Our schools are overrun with students that know arbitrary pieces of information and are unsure on how to apply it in their daily life. In determining the nature of education and what it entails, education as practical comprehension is crucial because it shows that education helps us to fulfill a purposeful concern as human beings. [6]

---

[6] See Heidegger's *Being and Time* for more on his notion of purposeful concern

Class Practice: Instant Insight!

I suggest to you a new class rule. This is more of a daily practice as opposed to an activity but effectual all the same. Regardless of your lesson, ensure that you provide learners with at least one solid, palatable, and directly applicable piece of information that they can use in their daily life ASAP. In providing your students with directly useful information, they will begin to value your class time more. This will increase student interest leading to higher student engagement.

For example, if I am teaching a class on college and career readiness, I will be sure to let learners know that it is important to have letters of recommendation and a personal statement. For an 11th grader, this is valuable insight that they can apply right away to start improving their academic portfolio. However, knowing that you should do a personal statement and actually using that knowledge to do it are two different things. Hence, the point of this exercise is to give them something applicable to their lives that they genuinely feel is useful. For another instance, consider I am delivering a seminar on stress management. One concrete takeaway that can be applied immediately is the concept of creating your own mental weather. I tell the kids that they have the ability to control their perception of what is happening to them by creating an aura using power phrases. Here are some examples of my own personal power phrases: "I own 10 schools in every state" "I am truly limitless" "I have no choice but to be great". These are little phrases that we can send to our subconscious mind to adjust our mental outlook, regardless of our current emotional state. While this is hard to master, this is certainly something that all of us - teacher and student alike - can greatly benefit from. The main takeaway here is that power phrases are something that can be used right away to help manage their stress and create a positive mindset.

Chapter 10

Progress

What is meant when we utter the term 'progress'? Simply put, progress can be thought of as a process of 'moving forward'. When you progress in something you start from one point – usually with less knowledge, aptitude, and experience – and you move to an upgraded point. Progress always involves upgrading, whether it is in knowledge, distance, skillset, etc. This moving forward is usually toward a specific goal to complete. Think about creating a new building from a vacant lot. The lot is littered with trees and debris. The workers begin to put up the first beams and gradually erect the building, adding pipes, bricks, and whatever is necessary to maintain the structure of the edifice. As the building comes closer to completion, the workers begin to create different levels of the building that will serve as floors with each floor containing rooms. Over time, the building moves through a process in which its status gradually improves. Each step in the process indicates a new level of progress attained for the erection of the building. Eventually, the building will reach the end of its creation and the building process will be complete; the building reaches 100% erection progression. But just because the building process is complete does not mean that the building cannot see more progress. Let's say this building was erected in 1948. As time passes, the building has some wiring issues and weather erosion which require some repairs and renovations to keep it running at optimal performance. In addition, the building may also need to update appliances to continue effectively accommodating its inhabitants. To state explicitly, the building is really in a constant state of progress until it ceases to be used by humanity. Tantamount to the constant progress of the building, progress has a similar function in education. In place of the building, think of a human that is undergoing a process of progression, and education replaces the builders. Just as the builders caused the progress of the building, education causes the progress of the individual. In reference to education, it is imperative to think of progress in this perpetual sense. Consider for a moment, the opposite reality in which education lacked the quality of progress. What would this look like? Let's explore this example using a form of micro education. Let's say the specialized craft is phlebotomy. A student seeks to learn the specifics of the field, the terminology, methodology, procedures, etc. After continued study of the field, the student aspires to one day be considered a world-class expert in phlebotomy. But how can she ever hope to achieve this status if she can never make it past the introductory concepts? How can she come to master the specialized techniques of the craft if she is unable to master the basic terms and methods? If she does not create a stable foundation of phlebotomy maxims from which to build from, how can she hope to understand the more profound concepts of the discipline? Thus, it stands to reason that in order to move forward in her quest to be a phlebotomy expert, she must first absorb and retain initial concepts and use this elementary knowledge as a launch pad to the advanced concepts. Devoid of progress, she will never make it past the entry-level concepts. In order to achieve progress, she must absorb and retain information and use these details to aid in gaining further practical comprehension on the subject. This initial absorption and retention of information is what sets the foundation for progress. This idea of foundationalism is a critical aspect of progress in relation to education because without a stable foundation, progress cannot be made and one's education cannot be built. Likewise, a building without a stable foundation will eventually collapse; in addition, a building of this nature will have a lower chance of seeing true progress because instead of spending time to advance the building's structure, time will be spent correcting issues regarding the poor foundation.

I mentioned that in reference to education progress should be conceived in a perpetual sense. Why must progression be an ongoing process in education? Very simply, education without consistent progress leads to a concept that I have termed stunted education. The notion of stunted education involves individuals who have reached a certain point of their educational development and decided that they no longer need to seek out new information because they are comfortable navigating the world with their current practical comprehension of it. This phenomenon is present in today's society and is detrimental for a few reasons. First, it prevents people from seeking out new information. This lack in the desire to acquire further knowledge is based in the belief that one has either: obtained enough knowledge to interact with their environment, or that one has gained enough experience through their lifetime in the world and they are certain of what works. Next, this characteristic antiquates one's practical comprehension and knowledge of the world. Let's explore an example of this stunted education in action. Recall the idea of macro-education which is comprised of one's general knowledge and ability. Consider the macro-education of an older lady, one who relies on old habits that worked in the past and is set in her methods of navigating life. This elder is content with what she already knows and has little to no desire to start varying her patterns of experiencing life. What is the cause of the lack of desire? One could speculate that maybe she fears change and does not want to take a risk on something that might not work when she has the option to use a method that is certain to be effectual. Consider the old woman who is used to conducting bank transactions via an in-person banking location. She is accustomed to traveling from her home to the bank in order to complete a transaction. This method always worked and she is pleased with it. However, as the times change technology makes banking more convenient. Where you once had to embark on an excursion to the bank, you now can address most of your banking needs through online banking or a mobile device. However, the old woman is distrustful of using technology for banking because of the fraudulent activity that could occur. She never displays her card or banking information on the internet or over the phone because she is afraid her information may be compromised. Although this does have the potential to occur, it may not be as likely to happen as she might believe. Her fear of taking a risk with an unknown path prevents her from taking advantage of a new and improved way of navigating the world. Although online banking is a much more convenient and faster way to handle transactions, adherence to old maneuvers and fear of fraudulent activity deters her from its benefits. This example shows how being content with an obsolete method of action can cause one to abdicate the opportunity for more efficient ways of experiencing the world.

Using micro-education, let's explore another example illustrating how stunted education can affect one's lived experience. Suppose there is a young skateboarder named Jon. He is 13 years of age and he has just started learning how to ride his board. He practices almost every day, and in 6 months, he is able to do some basic maneuvers such as an ollie, a kick turn, and a shuv-it. For those of you who may not be familiar with skating, these tricks are the equivalent to the elementary skills we learn when we first begin any new class. In terms of gaining further progress, these abilities are the necessary foundations to learn more advanced techniques. However, upon learning these moves Jon begins to feel comfortable performing only the skills that he knows that he will land with two feet. After 1 year from Jon's inception of skating, he still practices consistently and yet only knows a handful of tricks. This is due to his half-hearted practice methods. Aside from the easy tricks that he is able to perform, each attempt that he makes with an advanced trick always ends with him landing with one foot. Jon would throw the board into a perfect rotation, but he always landed with only his front foot on the board. Fast forward to when Jon is 20 years old and still skating. Still, he only knows basic tricks despite his time spent on the board. What is the cause of this clear lack of progress? In the last example of stunted education, the old woman did not want to use online banking because she was afraid of fraudulent activity. In other words, she did not feel comfortable; she did not want to leave her comfort zone because of the fear of taking a risk. With Jon, the notion of staying in one's comfort zone is also present here. More specifically, the main cause of Jon's stunted education is the fact that he is afraid to fall and in essence, afraid to fail. Ever since he learned to ride, he had a strong aversion of falling. As he went on with skateboarding, even though he was able to acquire a few modest abilities, his fear of falling ultimately caused his education of skateboarding to lack any true luster. Like any sport, skateboarding requires one to fail profusely before harnessing a proper technique. In essence, failure is instructive in that it is designed for us to learn how to perfect our methods using the learning method of trial and error. Due to its importance in relation to learning, failure will be the final section to be discussed in regard to the essentials of education.

Since things in our experience are constantly changing and developing, it is unwise to rely solely on a single set of ideas for too long. Our understanding of the world will soon become obsolete if we are not constantly adding to our knowledge, awareness, and practical comprehension. After exploring progress in relation to education, we can conclude that progress is a process of moving forward and the gaining of new abilities. The function of progress in education is the creation of foundations. From these foundations we can seek to expand our knowledge and practical comprehension and it is from these foundations that progress is made possible. However, if we antiquate ourselves by never gaining new abilities or if we mentally remain in the past, then progression in education cannot be realized. Progress is necessary in education because without it we would remain intellectually stagnant in an ever-changing reality.

Activity: Progress Planner

Given the importance of making progress on the path to improvement, it will be vital to help our learners with tracking their growth toward a goal. The chart below consists of an epic goal, stepping-stones, and an action plan. In simple terms, an epic purpose is a huge goal or mission that one is compelled to fulfill. This is your very reason for existing on this planet. This goal is often out of reach for the goal setter. Stepping-stones, as the name implies, are smaller missions that will bring you closer to your epic purpose. The action plan consists of the daily actions that you will take TODAY to begin bringing this epic purpose into reality. While this is good for the students, I encourage you to set these goals for yourself as well. Really gamify your progress planner and make it fun! In identifying your epic purpose and your progress toward it, you will find that you will begin to move with more certainty and clarity.

Example

To start, determine your personal calling, end goal, or major life purpose. Below I have provided my own personal example in hopes it will help you to identify your own. You will notice that I have written it in the present tense, as if I have already completed it although I have yet to do so. This helps to solidify my belief in its possibility, making it more achievable in my mind.

Epic Purpose: I have uprooted the common core curriculum and rebuilt it on principles of Humanization and Organic Intelligence.

Stepping-Stones: To achieve this, I will…

- Write a book on education and school change

- Connect with 20 community organizations in my neighborhood and offer to provide life-based enrichment

- Create video content on mentality building and education reform

Action Plan: Finally, you want to write down the day-to-day actions that will move you closer to your life mission. Let's say that you are making an action plan for Monday. It can look something like this:

- Call 5 community organizations and offer my services

- Complete 2 chapters of the book project

- Record a podcast episode and make 2 Instagram posts

In the progress planner, the epic purpose serves as your fuel and direction. With a laudable goal, you will find yourself moving with certainty and enthusiasm because you are striving toward something that truly matters to you.

The stepping-stones help to further guide your actions and keep your attention on what will aid in achieving your mission.

Finally, in setting a daily action plan you are exercising both discipline and effective usage of your time. With consistency in your efforts, this will pay off greatly in the long run. But you must actively apply it!

Now its your turn! Using the previous directions, fill out the following chart and create your own progress planner.

 For maximum results, be as detailed as possible in your vision for your epic purpose. The bigger and more specific your goal, the more staying power and velocity you will showcase in bringing that mission to fruition.

Action Plan	Stepping Stones	Epic Purpose

Chapter 11

Failure

Many people view failure as a negative event; they perceive it as something undesirable and to be avoided. Unfortunately, this viewpoint of failure is unhealthy because in eschewing failure, we are depriving ourselves of a crucial element necessary in our path to improvement. As we explore failure and its relation to education, we will examine its various components and determine why it is imperative to disavow the implicit fear of failure. In his 10x Rule, Cardone presents an interesting perception on fear. Contrary to popular view, Cardone writes "fear is the great indicator on where to go next" (Cardone, 2011). This is a beautiful statement because instead of trying to avoid fear, this outlook helps the person to use fear to their advantage. More specifically, fear is your brain's way of informing you on the presence of a new situation, one that is outside of your comfort zone. This is a prime opportunity for growth because it is outside this zone where you will meet your best self.

Failure as Instruction

For many individuals, public speaking is a nerve-racking experience. Standing in front of a myriad of eyes staring directly at you and waiting for you to take the lead of the discussion can certainly be a daunting responsibility. If you wish to effectively give a speech or presentation, it requires you to behave in a manner that is intelligible, competent, and comfortable. Due to this responsibility, many people become intimidated because they do not wish to embarrass themselves. It is a situation such as this where the fear of failure often stunts your performance. During my undergraduate career in college, I took a course on public speaking skills. Naturally, the focus of the class was to improve our ability to speak in front of a crowd. Unlike my classmates, I enjoyed this atmosphere and I eagerly absorbed all the information I could. In addition to my own learning, I watched others and how they interacted in class during the various exercises we engaged in. Although our class score was not on the line during these practical activities, the social failure of embarrassment was a veritable possibility. The activity in question required students to give a persuasive speech on a topic that was assigned only 10 minutes prior. Since many people had an apprehensive attitude toward public speaking and were unfamiliar with the information on which they had to present, this exercise proved challenging for most of the class. To give an idea on our collective performance, some students would stumble over their words, one would take extended pauses, and others would tend to fidget, unsure of how to incorporate their bodies into the presentation. Overall, most of the students ended the exercise in social failure. At the end of the activity, the professor brought out a small rolling table with a projector superimposed upon it. He also had a camera set up in the rear of the room that was recording each of the students' comportment as we presented. As we watched the playbacks, we were shocked to realize how we looked as we stood up front. Many of the students stated they didn't even realize what they were doing most of the time while giving their presentation. The relevance of this is the fact that we didn't notice the specific details that caused us to be so awkward and tenuous in persuasion. The professor went over each film of every student with the class and analyzed them one-by-one. As he went through the playbacks, we were made aware of where we were inept and he advised us on how it could be fixed. Thus by us failing, being made aware of how we failed and how to remedy it, we were placed on a path to improvement. But what if our fear of failure had consumed us at the inception of the activity in such a way that made us not participate? What if we never gave the presentation but instead decided to remain in the 'social safe zone' where the grip of embarrassment cannot reach? In this rendition of the scenario, how could the path to improvement ever be paved if we didn't take the first step of trial and failure? In terms of public speaking, we would have little idea on what to improve because we do not have a specimen from which to analyze and make adjustments on. Hence, failure cannot instruct us if we never engage in it; for it to teach us something, we must experience it firsthand. Clearly, we would not reach the path to improvement in public speaking if we never took the first step of the journey. But most importantly, in never making an attempt, we are robbed of the opportunity to fail. To restate, the adherence to the 'social safe zone' steals the opportunity to fail. Yes, the *opportunity* to fail. In order to improve at anything, failure is necessary at one point or another. Since it can show an individual what they specifically need to work on, failure can be one of the greatest exposers of knowledge if we weren't always so quick to evade it. It follows that failure serves an instructive purpose in our lives. This does not mean that we should actively be trying to fail in our endeavors, for in doing this we will not have an accurate assessment of our true performance or knowledge of what needs to be modified. Rather, when one's hard efforts are met with failure one should use this instance as admonishment on what to do or not do. In addition, failure is instructive because it shows us how to be creative and resourceful. When one approach doesn't work, out of necessity to achieve a goal, we find another way to more appropriately fit the task. Failure is a birthplace for ideas and it is through resilience of repeated failure that grit and innovation are forged and sharpened. In essence, we all have the capacity to further develop attributes about ourselves. Carol Dweck explains this mental orientation toward improvement as 'growth mindset' which is, "…based on the belief that your basic qualities are things that you can cultivate through your efforts, strategies, and help from others...everyone can change and grow through application and experience" (Dweck, Ch. 1). Consider my niece, Autumn, who is ten years of age; she recently learned how to play chess. Eager to know if I knew how to play as well, she challenged me to a match. I accepted her challenge, she set up the board, and we proceeded to the game. After a few minutes of playing, she was in checkmate. We played again and a similar result ensued. This repeated a few more times and after the fifth time, I asked, "do you realize why you are losing?" She replied, "No, I'm trying to take your pieces but you keep stopping me every time I make a plan." I responded, "Taking pieces is only one part of the game, in order to win you must use those pieces in a specific way to trap the king." Even though she was constantly losing, she was determined to finally put me in checkmate for once. This desire pushed her to keep trying despite her failures. We started to make a small habit of playing chess on occasion and when we play I can see her begin to shift her methods and tactics for the game. Although she still loses each match we play, I can see her style switching from simply capturing as many pieces as possible to finding ways to make me move into precarious situations. Her ability to adjust her approach based off repeated failures is indicative of the instructive quality of failure. Analogous to trial and error, failure is something that teaches us via our personal experience. Thus, one of the functions of failure is to instruct the learner on what to initiate or avoid as well as inspire within them the necessity to adapt.

Failure as Recollection

In terms of education, failure and memory play a specific relationship involving memory recall. Of many things, failure can often involve fixation on the memory and feeling of one's failure in any given event in their life. This memory of failure can be debilitating - which leads to fear of failure - or empowering - which leads to using failure as fuel - depending on the person experiencing it. For those that fixate on wishing that some past events in their lives would have unfolded differently, they are robbing themselves of the present moment and of all its opportunities. It is evident that changing the past is an impossible feat, for if it wasn't, I myself would have surely mastered its arts. Simply put, dwelling on something that is a physical impossibility only serves to drain one's spirit.

Fear of failure

Fixation on past shortcomings can lead to fear of failure in the present as well as the future. Due to the regret of not achieving a goal and all of the negative articles that accompany this – i.e. ridicule, demotion, loss of resources, etc. - the person never wants to experience the feeling again. Cardone mentions a similar notion which he refers to as 'retreat', "Retreaters are those who take actions in reverse, probably in order to avoid negative experiences that they imagine may come as a result of taking action...He or she has experienced results that they did not perceive as fruitful and is now avoiding taking further actions to prevent failing again" (Cardone, 2011). This poor experience was so unpleasant that they now seek to avoid the feeling at all costs. This is termed the fear of failure; it is caused by the trauma of a past failure or succession of past failures that one feels deep regret and shame toward. This fear of failure is extremely pernicious to education. This causes people to stay in their comfort zone and deters them from learning because they are too afraid to explore uncharted territories; for individuals of this nature, it is too risky and dangerous to leave the zone of comfort and predictability. They are afraid to make mistakes because someone may ridicule them or they may embarrass themselves and 'stand out' from the crowd. Unfortunately, this mindset of 'playing it safe' and avoiding uncomfortable situations is inculcated into the minds of the youth from the time they were able to take their first independent steps. An occurrence of a vigilant mother telling her little girl to be careful while running at the park to avoid scraping her knee is a classic instance of the mother unwittingly chaining her daughter to the "safe zone". Although the mother's intentions are the safety of her child, she is unknowingly shaping her daughter to view the world in a way that may limit her full potential and this shaping will influence her behavior in future events. Think of the child when she matures into an adult. She experienced an upbringing in which she was constantly told to be cautious, reserved, and conservative. In addition, her mother is constantly having her avoid pain and unpleasant things. This will no doubt affect her comportment in her adult life. As a result, it is more likely that she will avoid pain and unpleasant situations when she grows into an adult, instead of dealing with them head on. If this were to happen, she would be at a disadvantage with emotionally taxing situations and other problems if she has little to no experience with them due to a shielded child rearing. In Rousseau's Emile he writes, "…He must be familiarized with peril in order that he may not be affected by it…" (Rousseau, 96). Thus, in order to be able to deal with challenging situations, we need to be accustomed to doing so by doing it repeatedly and gaining practical comprehension of it. Let's suppose this girl, we will call her Jackie, grows up to be a reserved non-risk-taker. Picture her at her office job in which she is working long hours and she would like a raise. In order to obtain her objective, she needs to talk to her boss about what she desires. However, since Jackie is so used to not leaving the "safety zone" of risk-taking she finds it intimidating to request a raise because there is a chance of being rejected. She is afraid of rejection because it is one of those uncomfortable articles attributed with failure. In addition, she fears the embarrassment of her efforts being met with inconclusive results. To allude to the playground example earlier, she doesn't wish to 'fall down and scrape her knee', in other words she would rather just stay silent in the safe zone and continue work as usual because in doing so she would take no risk and experience no unpleasant feelings. This perception of failure as phenomena to be avoided only serves to perpetuate individuals of average mentality and mediocre improvement levels. Fearing failure is tantamount to fearing nourishment of one's body. Imagine a person with an aversion to eating; how would they persist in life? Would not their body decay away and leave only the feeble remains of a once vital being? Even if they did not perish, their physique would indeed be tenuous. Although one will not physically perish because of fear of failure, the magnitude is of equal importance. With education, one's physical life is not on the line but rather their life as an intellectual being; the life of their essence and spirit of uniqueness and creativity is what is at stake. Just as the body will die if we do not receive food due to fear of it, our improvement as a human will cease to exist if we fear the very thing that seeks to nourish it. Thus, fearing failure is the same as fearing education, since it is through failure that we can learn and enhance ourselves. And by fearing education, we fear the process that enables us to become closer to the best version of ourselves. Hence, it stands to reason that fixating on failure in this way is deleterious.

Failure as Fuel and Motivation

In contrast with the fear of failure, there are individuals that use failure as motivation to complete their desired mission. When one uses their past experiences, emotions, and losses as a solemn reminder of which paths to avoid on their quest for improvement, this serves to aid them in their journey because it brings them closer to the right path. Using these memories and emotions as fuel to find success grants that person a sense of resolve and empowerment. Think of a teenager giving a performance for a talent show. This teen, Martha, decides to play the violin as her skill. However, during her performance, she makes numerous mistakes and afterwards many of her peers poke fun at her for messing up in a public setting. For Martha, this can affect her in one of two ways: 1) Due to the uncomfortable occurrence of making a mistake in front of others and the ridicule she received, she could be deterred from ever playing the violin in public again. This type of response is much in line with the fear of failure outlook that we previously discussed. 2) The other way in which this could unfold is by Martha feeling a strong urge of determination and self-efficacy; having people doubt her made her want to prove them wrong and made her want to prove to herself that she could do better. This second stance is what is referred to as failure as fuel and motivation. In the first instance Martha would have just given up altogether and that would not help to improve her violin ability or her public performance. Thus, it stands to reason that the second outlook proves more beneficial to her because instead of using her circumstances as a reason to quit, she uses them as a reason to persist and thrive. Imagine the benefit this second mentality could yield on the education of the youth. In essence, the youth cannot be expected to automatically perceive failure in this way. In order to have resilient warriors who are not silenced by failure, those that reveal information to the youth should cultivate the desire to overcome one's failure in order to reach an improved practical comprehension. So how can we do this? For starters, it is essential to encourage students that it is **OKAY** to fail. Given the way the grading system is set up, teachers are motivated to deter students from failure. In schools, failure is seen as bad and shameful. You are not considered a good student for failing. However, if teachers were not pressured by the system to produce competitive students with high test scores, more time could be spent on organic learning, Socratic methods, and *practicing how to learn from failure* in **and** out of the classroom. Consequently, the activity below is designed to help both you and your students become intimately familiar with failure and rejection so you can begin to mitigate the paralysis caused by fear of failure.

Activity: Fight the Fear Challenge

Born from Jia Jang's book Rejection Proof, this challenge can be conducted both in the classroom and assigned as an optional take home fun goal. [7]

* Quick note, I strongly encourage you to do this challenge yourself before doing it with your class or at home with your children. If you can be comfortable facing your own fears effectively, it will help you significantly in facilitating this exercise. Also, be sure to Fight the Fear with the class once you finally introduce it to them, it will make them more inclined to engage! *

The challenge is very simple, your job is to assign the students the task of actively seeking out failure. Yes, I know this sounds counterintuitive, but hear me out. Have the students make a list of personal and school activities that make them uncomfortable, uncertain, and afraid. Now within appropriateness and reason, have them select 1 item from that list that they can try during class. By the way, this activity can be active during normal class

---

[7] In Rejection Proof, Jang embarks on a quest of courage and personal development. In order to overcome his fear of rejection, he initiates a 100-day challenge where he actively seeks out rejection. From asking ridiculous requests, to trying to get free meals, he really stretches the barriers of what we would normally consider acceptable. This is an interesting idea to adapt for the classroom because it gives students the opportunity to become accustomed to failure and rejection so that they will not be so afraid of it all the time.

time, you won't need to reserve a whole period for this. Given the nature of this activity, I understand that there will certainly be aversion to participation. So as the educator, it would be wise for you to co-create an incentive to promote student engagement. Together with your students, find out things they want, things that interest them, things they want to do in life and in school. After carefully creating incentives that inspire the kids, you can begin the activity. Perhaps your incentive goes like this: Whoever faces three of their fears for 5 days this week will be rewarded with the ability to choose the next class lesson, class game, event, or trip. If there are multiple achievers, then you will just have to plan multiple days of student-selected activities, which is good because it actively involves student voice. There can be other ways to incentivize your learners and you can conduct this in anyway you choose, this is only one example of how to set this up. The more creative you are, the more possibilities you can surmise. Perhaps offer funds, scholarships, interview time, free trip to visit a campus or anything else that is applicable, meaningful, and relevant to the lives of your learners.

Example of how this would work:

Step 1: Students write down 6 items they feel they are not good at, afraid of, or uncomfortable to do. The list will include 3 personal and 3 academic challenges.

Step 2: Students select one item from the list, and during class they will be tasked with attempting this action. For example, if a student writes down on his academic list that raising his hand is a source of fear or he feels he may fail by giving the wrong answer, then this is the action that he will be challenged to overcome.

Step 3: After setting the rules of the game, the educator will have a list of the academic challenge that each student has selected. It is up to both the teacher and student to keep a track of the completion of the Fear Challenge. At the end of each class, teachers will make a note on their list if someone completed their challenge. In addition, students will make a note to the teacher if they completed the challenge. To help inoculate against false reports, the students will also be placed in trios or pairs of accountability buddies to verify with the teacher if someone did indeed seek to fight the fear. In the end, this challenge also relies on an honor system, so the way in which this activity is introduced is paramount. Be light-hearted, open, and honest when introducing this activity. Paint a picture of how this is super fun and beneficial. Most importantly, lead by example! Be sure to play the game alongside your learners as this will help to break the ice. For example, in my own teaching experience I have a few Spanish speakers in my seminars. By attempting to communicate with them in Spanish, a language I am only 32% fluent in, this is my way of facing my own fears and doing something outside of my zone of comfort. I even made a fool of myself by mispronouncing a word! This really got the students laughing! The point is, by them watching me deal with being uncomfortable in order to improve, they are more inclined to participate as well.

Chapter 12

Humanization and Organic Intelligence: A Brighter Future

Now that we have explored some important aspects and essential qualities of education, I want to outline the school climate that can be created if we centered on these qualities as the true foundation of our American school system. As stated many times in this book, our current education system focuses too heavily on competition, academic excellence, and the creation of factory workers. Schools teach kids how to read, write, and duplicate the intelligence of others with less focus on actually applying their knowledge and sharpening their own creativity. With this focus on duplication, it is hard for students to cultivate originality and they make less progression toward their full humanity because they are stuck thinking that there are only two ways to exist in the world, as a worker and consumer. This is the great lie of the American school system. Given the heavy focus on test-taking, ranking and all the pressure that accompanies this, students are often afraid to fail. As discussed in the last chapter, this is pivotal because in avoiding failure, we simultaneously avoid progression and improvement which only serves to ensure our long-term failure in life. With these problems permeating schools, it is vital that we begin a shift in the way we conceive of education, teaching, learning, and what is considered worth exploring. Enter Humanization and Organic Intelligence. (HOI)

The premise of this approach is to cultivate the full humanity of not only students, but all education stakeholders. This is done through keen implementation of: life-based curriculum, place-based learning, altruism, interdependence, and whole-person education. I am currently crafting a whole book on HOI Principles, but I will briefly outline it here.

Life Enrichment

This is at the forefront of HOI Principles. As we have explored, one of the major mistakes of schooling is the hyper focus on only a select few aspects of life. Let's get real, our life consists of much more than just exams, math, reading, and science. However, given their prominence in schools one could be led to believe that these are the most important aspects of our existence. Debunking this false belief, HOI prioritizes the accumulation of life capacities as opposed to only academic excellence. Centering life skills as the main focus of school, HOI explores topics such as: facing your fears, spirituality, financial literacy, philosophy, emotional intelligence, active listening, goal setting, success mindset, and so much more. The goal here is not to create top students or top workers, it is to cultivate humans that are intrinsically motivated to consistently developing their full potential. In implementing HOI, it will be possible for more people to follow their purpose and lead fulfilling lives in which they are striving to become the best version of themselves while inspiring others to do the same.

Place-Based Learning

In our contemporary educational situation, we are so accustomed to traveling to a classroom and conducting the majority of schooling *within* four walls. Save for the few times students get to embark on field trips outside, for some reason it would appear schools believe that learning can only occur in a classroom. The implicit message sent to the youth is "learning is reserved for school." Given the way classes are conducted now, lecture styled with students in rows facing forward where many students are treated as information deposit boxes, it isn't a surprise that students may feel disengaged. In essence, our schools are turning learners into allotted educatists, individuals that limit their orientation to learning. It is because of the repetitive, dry, and unentertaining nature of the physical classroom that HOI curriculum employs placed-based learning in a radical way. Due to this disengaging class layout and instruction style, HOI seeks to flip the traditional model of schooling on its head. Instead of learning about the world from the walls of the classroom, students will directly engage in the world AS their classroom. To state differently, class will be conducted in various locations in the local city or town throughout the day, on a daily basis. While this may sound like a field trip every day, the purpose will not be solely for fun or recreation. Given the fact the children are people first and exist in the real world, would it not be sensible for them to learn their lessons *from* the real world? To use the earlier example of China, there is only but so much you can glean by simply learning the theoretics of a place or item. I believe this is why stereotypes and prejudice are so rampant. We have been miseducated by school, parents, etc. and we had limited to no direct experience with the topic we are being revealed to. If we had more consistent direct experience with the subjects, people, and places we study and are told about through daily life, it would yield a more tangible and informed experience. Your understanding of the thing would certainly be augmented if you have direct contact with it. In other words, if you want to truly learn about China, go to China! Hence, HOI provides students with a direct frame of reference from which to garner images, data, and understanding. In directly interacting with the real world, opportunities to educate on life skills have no choice but to emerge. For instance, consider one of your activities of the day is billiards. You are with your class of 9th grade freshman and you notice that during the game, one of your students is becoming frustrated because she can't make her shot and she begins to think she's just naturally bad at playing pool.[8] This is a

---

[8] Dweck would note this as a classic example of the fixed mindset at work.

prime moment to expose her to the benefits of determining the right approach while being persistent. If you can build a bridge to her and show her that you understand her situation, she may be more inclined to receive your advice. For example, you could say something like, "Hey when I was just starting out, I used to always hit the ball off the table! But with practice, I began to get better." Then, you mention to her that it's not that she is naturally bad at pool, it's just that she needs to make sure she is using the right techniques. With the other students watching, you can show her various ways of holding the stick, positioning her body, and adjusting her stance so that she will increase her chances of a successful shot. Now you may wonder why I chose billiards as an example. While some may think this is a random and useless activity, I believe that this is an effective way to reveal learners to geometry in action, practicing prediction using angles and trajectory, planning, and persistence to improve. Furthermore, this is a hands-on way to get students involved and engaged in the class and building relationships. Ultimately, as illustrated with Dale's Cone of Learning, it is far easier to remember activities and time periods in which we were directly engaged in, where we took action, and where we participated. Using this truth as a launch pad, HOI prioritizes direct involvement over distant 2nd hand lecture.

Altruism

Our current world has a strong shortage of superheroes. What do I mean by this? Take a look at every superhero on TV, comic, or video game. Beside some supernatural ability they possess, this person is often characterized as someone that puts millions of other people's needs before their own, often times putting their own life at risk to save another. In addition, they express deep and genuine care for EVERY person they come in contact with; they really want to protect others and make a difference in their lives. It is this altruistic capacity to care for others, regardless if you know them or not, that the dearth of authentic care is evident. In our American society, we place heavy value on the individual and as a result, we tend to become a bit egotistic when it comes to caring about others outside of our circle of family and friends. Many times, we only express care in another if there is something that we can get out of them in return. Let's face it, do you genuinely *care* about the random person down the street? Do you authentically care about them as if they were your mom, friend, or lover? Unfortunately, many of us would probably say no to this question, myself included. It is not that we wish bad for that person or wish them ill, it is simply that we are so accustomed to only being concerned with ourselves and our immediate circle. Our upbringing and early experiences have conditioned us to have limited to no care for random strangers. So why does this matter? Well, there are over 7 billion people in the world and over 300 million in the United States alone. It has been said countless times, "Alone you are strong, but together you are unstoppable." I agree with this conventional wisdom because no matter how much one person can get done alone, they can multiply their efforts if they partner up with someone of equal or greater skill. Just think about the amazing skyscrapers humanity has erected. If it weren't for an elite team of builders, designers, architects, and engineers coming together and working as a collective, we would not have fancy skyscrapers today. Look at cars, computers, or any other advanced technology on this planet. A group of people had to team up to achieve a common project goal. Now let's look at the project of life. Where our project goal was building a computer, our project goal here is developing and supporting our full humanity. Like crafting a skyscraper or supercomputer, this is a massive goal that requires the input of a team. Just think, how effective would a person be at making a supercomputer if they had to do all the work themselves? What if that one person is only good at software engineering but has no idea on how to do the hardware setup? Or if they were really good in designing cosmetic features but have no idea how to physically build a motherboard? This would prove extremely challenging for this person if not next to impossible. Similarly, we are currently engaged in the massive project of life with extremely limited team members. We have to realize that as humans we are all on the same team. We all want to be healthy, we all want to be happy, we all want to feel important. These are basic universal truths of the human condition. However, instead of focusing on what we have in common, we tend to place most of our attention on the things that divide us. In addition, we even create ways to further segregate ourselves from each other, think division between boys and girls in schools, the segregation laws back in the 20th century, income levels, etc. Back in ancient times when humanity still had to physically fight everyday to survive, it was apropos for us to differentiate our tribe from others because we needed to protect our loved ones. In today's time, this tribalism is still very much alive and well. However, there is no longer a need to be so tribal and territorial. In fact, in today's society this type of thinking severely limits our possibilities. The time is long overdue for us to band together not only as a nation, but more importantly as a species. Imagine the possibility we could have as humans if we genuinely cared for one another and TRULY wanted the best for each other? How would our world look if we ALL got *really* excited when we see others winning? How would our world look if we didn't experience hate or resentment toward others, but instead we became inspired to help them to achieve greatness as well as achieve the same for ourselves? I believe humanity would be much closer to reaching the next rung of existence. Hence, HOI Principles seeks to create superheroes with a superfluous care for every person they meet.

Whole-Person Approach

Science, Technology, Math, Engineering. Commonly referred to as STEM, this program and its subjects are often popularized as main things students should know, along with language arts of course. With the spotlight centered on these areas, schools send an implicit message: this is what's really important. Many kids, parents, and teachers have loss sight of the other essentials of humanity. The human person is not composed merely of quadratic formulas, phonetic phrases, or advanced technology. Given that we place heavy value on these in schools however, a different song is written here. To break free of the malady of neoliberal education, it is critical for schools to adopt HOI Principles. Incorporating the whole-child approach of education, HOI expands the idea by including real world activities centered on unlocking the Limitless Self.[9] So along with interactive sessions of hands-on math, reading, and science, students will learn about intuition, spirit energy, managing one's own emotions, public speaking, empathy, success mindset, and improvisation. I know I have mentioned this before, but it is absolutely imperative for schools to prioritize the other essential aspects of the human person. The ability to know why you feel the way you do about an emotion and then not allow it to dominate your behavior is such a valuable life skill. Or knowing how to handle rejection. Schools never teach that, if anything they teach you how to *avoid* rejection and failure. For another capacity, think of how useful it would be if we taught learners how to create a success mindset where they can produce mental and physical prosperity. The point I am making here is not that STEM and language arts are bad. They are just executed in an ineffectual manner and require

---

[9] The Limitless Self is a term I created as an ideal to strive for. It can be thought of as one's true self, unhampered by doubt or negative aura. This will be defined in greater detail in my next book, HOI Principles.

additional subjects in order to better service the child. To foster the full development of the child, we must add some new priorities to our school roster and unlearn the harmful beliefs of fixed mindset, segregation, individuality, and hierarchy that have been imposed on this nation and our school system.

Application of Ability

HOI Principles are heavily centered on being able to apply what you know and can do. So in this approach, each and every class conducted in HOI curriculum will include imparting at least ONE piece of useful and immediately applicable information. For example, consider we are having a class on financial literacy in which we are discussing investing. The main goal of today's class is to learn about cryptocurrency by studying different coins, learning some metrics, and opening up the trading view application. An example of a concrete lesson that high school students could implement immediately is this: save to invest, don't save to save. Once you begin saving to invest, be sure to withdraw 30-40% of your allowance or income with the goal of investing it in the future.[10] Think of this in another scenario where students are learning about interpersonal communications. In addition to learning about tonality, body language, and voice inflection, the concrete takeaway they can begin applying from this topic could be: ensure that you try to understand someone before offering your viewpoint. Stephen Covey mentions this idea as one of the principles of highly effective people, "Seek first to understand, then to be understood" (Covey, 1989). Now when students have interpersonal interactions, they will have a practical tool in their communications belt that will make engaging with others

---

[10] This concept of save to invest and withdraw 30-40% of income derives from my studies of Grant Cardone's Millionaire Playbook: How to Get Super Rich

smoother, provided they apply what they learned. All in all, HOI seeks to create people that know how to synergize their understanding and implement their knowledge effectively in ways that benefit themselves, others, and the environment.

Activity: Learner Lessons

HOI Principles seeks to implement altruism, interdependence, and the whole-child approach as THE foundation of education, not as an add-on initiative. Ideally, once HOI has its own established school system, we can use these ideas as the crux of our inquiry. For now, given that I know many of you are teaching within a limited context, I have adapted this activity to be used in conjunction with current practices. One staple notion of HOI is valuing student voice. This activity is designed to get students actively involved in the classroom process by selecting the next topic to be discussed as a group. So the activity goes as follows:

Step 1 – Pose the Question

At the top of your class, ask the students, "If you had the ability to choose, which topics would you want to learn in school?" or you can phrase it like, "If you had to decide what activities or areas of study that we did everyday, what would they be?"

This will get them thinking about what interests them, and in turn they are telling you what will keep them engaged. For teachers with time restrictions in your class due to current teach-to-the-test models I understand that this may be a bit daunting because it will be taking away from coverage time. But let's face it, much of the test material that we are teaching students is not the most useful and they probably aren't fully paying attention anyway. So if we are going to have class time, why not use it on something that could increase student engagement? In addition, if executed right and the proper connections are drawn between the students' request and the coverage material, we can kill 2 birds with one stone – increasing student engagement while learning test material.

Step 2 – Record and Collect Answers

Once you have students brainstorming things they would want to learn, the next step is to have each student take out a small piece of paper and write down at least 2 of their ideas. Then, collect these papers and save them as your Learner Lesson Pile.

Step 3 - Explore the Learner Lessons

Okay so let's do some quick math. Say you have 21 students with 2 ideas each. That will provide you with 42 topics to explore. Now considering your current lesson plan and class time, I would suggest taking only 5 minutes at the start of each class to explore one of the student topics with the class. Also, if one 5-minute block is not enough time to talk about a topic, you can extend that topic into the beginning of the next class. In doing this, you are actively showing them that you not only value what they have to say, but that it is worth talking about. I understand I may receive some pushback for this suggestion due to strict class time that needs to be spent covering material. But let me ask you something, which is more important? Arbitrary test material? Or rich and authentic student engagement?

Step 4 – Make it Make Sense

Now some of you may be wondering, "So where does the rich and authentic student engagement come in?" Let's say a student provides a topic that on the outset seems irrelevant and of no value. Say the topic is a television show or their deep interest in basketball. On the face of it, this has nothing to do with your class, which is history. Your job is to weave in student interest with the learning material making it relevant and accessible to them. So for instance let's say a student says "I want to be a top basketball player". That's the first sentence to start the conversation from your Learner Lessons. You could start by asking them, "why do you want to do this?" After hearing them out and making them feel understood, you could then start drawing connections by suggesting "well if you want to be a top player, one good thing you could do is to go over the history of players in the past and start taking notes on how they got there." You can use their interest in basketball to make the point that it is always important to know your history regardless of the topic because it can inform your actions moving forward. Now later in the class, you can use the earlier conversation as a bridge for future understanding. For instance, "Remember how we said that in order to do well in basketball it would be good to study the history of the top players? Likewise, that is why we are studying the history of America, to see what worked, what didn't, and how we can improve moving forward, does that make sense?" This method of making it make sense will really help learners to see that many things in this universe are connected even though at first they may seem so separate.

Step 5 – Be Consistent

Once you start doing the Learner Lessons, stick with them! They are a fun way to jumpstart the class with higher student engagement and may make learners more receptive to your future messages.

Closing Thoughts

After exploring education and its various components, we can conclude that it is a multifaceted and invaluable asset to us as human beings. It is the instrument that sharpens us as individuals and allows us to explore the different elements of the world. It is what gives us guidance and direction in our lives. In regards to education, "Direction expresses the basic function, which tends at one extreme to become a guiding assistance...Direction involves a focusing and fixating of action..." (Dewey, 1916). In this section of his work, Dewey mentions how the proper notion of control is important in understanding the role of direction in achieving a desired result. As educators, parents, and school leaders, we must ensure that we are not exercising the pejorative social control over our children where we simply dictate what they do and expect them to blindly follow suit. Instead, the essence of education involves allowing a learner's positive control of themselves to emerge in such a way that will in turn foster an interdependent society. Further Dewey states, "To achieve internal control [for learners] through identity of interest and understanding is the business of education" (Dewey, 1916). Hence, it is crucial that as insight revealers, we keep our attention on helping students to discover and develop their understanding of the human experience. Moreover, education is the factor that provides the lens thru which we view the world and it shapes our personality. With education, we can improve ourselves in our own unique way and we can share this improvement with others. Education is the implement we use to know our environment and how to interact with it skillfully; it is our defense when others attempt to prevaricate or swindle. It is also the tool we utilize in order to influence the minds of others. Ultimately, it is the major device we use to thrive in our transient existence. Many people go through life as another sheep in a vast herd. In order to avoid mere existence, in order to truly thrive in life, one must educate - i.e. get better at something - themselves in *some* manner. This can take many forms; the form it takes depends on the person's desired goal. If they wish to influence others, then they must gain education in emotional intelligence and interpersonal communication. If one seeks to write a novel, they must practice creative writing and effective control over their given language. Overall, if one wants to achieve anything of notable consequence in the world, education is the means by which to accomplish their mission. Stated differently, if you want to do anything at a high-performance level, you must first learn it and improve upon it. There are some people that believe doing the bare minimum in their life is appropriate and acceptable; some may not have the desire to get better at anything at all. To those individuals, I give this brief message. While these people certainly have the freedom to live their life in a mediocre and simple manner devoid of self-improvement, I believe in doing this they do themselves and their human cohorts a grave injustice. Ultimately, to access our full potential in this world as humans, it is paramount for us to focus on improvement, forward movement, and working interdependently to achieve a more supportive and altruistic world. I believe together, we have the power to improve humanity and unlock our Limitless Self. We need only apply our insight as a collective unit. From one educator to another, let us rebuild schooling with the goal of creating a brighter future for education.

Stay Cultivating,

Robert Astwood

References

Biesta, G. (2017). The rediscovery of teaching. Routledge, Taylor & Francis Group

Cardone, G. (2011). The 10x rule: the only difference between success and failure. John Wiley & Sons.

Cattell, R. B. (1963). Theory of fluid and crystallized intelligence: A critical experiment. Journal of Educational Psychology, 54(1), 1–22. https://doi.org/10.1037/h0046743

Counts, G. S. (1982). Dare the school build a new social order? Southern Illinois University Press. With Preface by Wayne J. Urban

Covey, S. R. (1989). The 7 Habits of Highly Effective People. Running Press.

Dale, E. (1946). Audio-visual methods in teaching. The Dryden press.

Descartes, René, 1596-1650. (1993). Discourse on method ; and, Meditations on first philosophy. Indianapolis :Hackett Pub. Co.

Dewey, J. (2019). Democracy and education: an introduction to the philosophy of education. Bumbershoot Books.

Dweck, C. S. (2016). Mindset: the new psychology of success. Ballantine Books.

Heidegger, M. (2013). Being and time. Stellar Books.

Kohn, Alfie (2015). 2015 Education Conference: The Schools our Kids Deserve. The W. Edwards Deming Institute. https://www.youtube.com/watch?v=-Ts_SRJuEdw. YouTube

Lynch, M. (2017). Understanding Key Education Issues How We Got Here and Where We Go From Here. Taylor and Francis.

Rousseau, J.-J., & Foxley, B. (1921). Emile, or, Education. J.M. Dent & Sons.

www.ingramcontent.com/pod-product-compliance
Lightning Source LLC
Chambersburg PA
CBHW021942160426
43195CB00011B/1188